GAIN THE STRENGTH OF A CIRQUE PERFORMER, THE LEGS
OF A BALLET DANCER AND THE ABS OF A PILATES PRO

AERIAL PHYSIQUE
FIT

— JILL FRANKLIN —

Aerial Physique FIT
Copyright © 2017 Aerial Physique LLC
Photography By: TC Franklin Photography

All rights reserved. No part of this book may be reproduced, or transmitted in any form or by any means, without the prior written permission of Jill Franklin of Aerial Physique LLC.

Printed in the United States of America
ISBN-10: 0-692-82283-6
ISBN-13: 978-0-692-82283-8

DEDICATION

I dedicate this book to all who have a desire to learn, grow and become a better version of themselves. May this book help and inspire you to gain more strength, flexibility and confidence.

CONTENTS

Introduction 1

Core Program 16

Lower Body Program 66

Upper Body Program 102

Stretching Program 126

Acknowledgements 149

INTRODUCTION

Statistics show that exercising not only improves how the body moves on a daily basis, but it can also sharpen your focus and aid in keeping you in a positive mood. Perhaps the number one component is performing an exercise properly. The information, suggestions and images in this manual are designed to give you the strength of a cirque performer, the legs of a ballet dancer and the abs of a Pilates pro. In the following sections you will be introduced to principles, Pilates based concepts, stretching methods, human anatomy and fitness equipment you'll need. The specific and targeted exercises will challenge you physically and with patience and practice, you'll notice vast improvements in your core, upper and lower body strength and overall flexibility. Believe in yourself! Go for it!

INTRODUCTION
Dear Reader

Dear Reader:

I wrote this book because of YOU. We all have a hidden artist deep within. An artist, who will undoubtedly face challenges and set backs. It's those difficult times when the inner winner can and must birth itself into existence. It's called WILL POWER. You have the power to guide your thoughts, actions and goals. Only you can think them, only you can set them. My initial goal when I first began aerial was simple. I wanted to execute one pull-up. Yes, ONE.. PERFECT.. PULL-UP!

While it might sound like the most ridiculous goal, that one pull-up was my grand nemesis. As far back as I can remember, I would get sweaty armpits as a kid knowing I had to attend gym class. I would actually hang from the pull-up bar with arms overhead, unable to muster even the slightest of upward movement. Embarrassed? Indeed! I eventually passed gym class, but not the pull-up test.

But soon, I began to believe in my ability to reach a goal. I moved to New York City just after my 21st birthday to pursue dancing and acting on Broadway. Within 6 months the acting bug fizzled out and fitness kicked in. I never gave up the desire to become physically and mentally strong. With a background in ballet and a career in Pilates, I knew the dedication and discipline it takes to become excellent at a craft. I took my first aerial class in 2007 and I was hooked. It took me 6 more months but I finally completed my first pull-up.

My aim is to inspire you to persevere to tackle all of your goals in life. May the exercises in this book give you strength and confidence to achieve anything you set your mind to.

With gratitude & appreciation,

Jill Franklin

INTRODUCTION
About the Author

Jill Franklin is the founder of Aerial Physique. She is also a celebrity trainer and author of numerous books including *Beginners Guide to Aerial Silk, Intermediate Guide to Aerial Silk, Aerial Silks Coloring Book & Cirque Coloring Book* available on Amazon.com & Shopaerialphysique.com. She maintains a highly sought after You Tube channel and a web based video site, Aerial Physique TV. Jill is also a clothing designer with a line featuring the J-Boss Jumpsuit, specifically for aerial work! Jill has a certifiable Aerial Teacher Training Program here in the U.S. and is available around the world. Jill's teaching expertise enables instructors to better teach their own students, with innovative and exciting aerial silks skills.

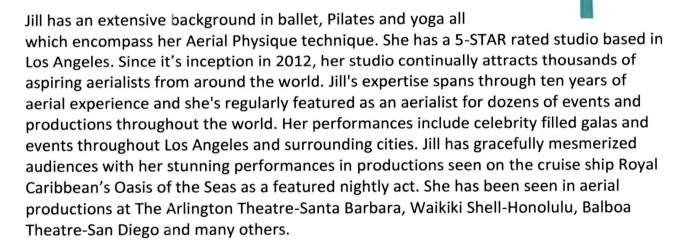

Jill has an extensive background in ballet, Pilates and yoga all which encompass her Aerial Physique technique. She has a 5-STAR rated studio based in Los Angeles. Since it's inception in 2012, her studio continually attracts thousands of aspiring aerialists from around the world. Jill's expertise spans through ten years of aerial experience and she's regularly featured as an aerialist for dozens of events and productions throughout the world. Her performances include celebrity filled galas and events throughout Los Angeles and surrounding cities. Jill has gracefully mesmerized audiences with her stunning performances in productions seen on the cruise ship Royal Caribbean's Oasis of the Seas as a featured nightly act. She has been seen in aerial productions at The Arlington Theatre-Santa Barbara, Waikiki Shell-Honolulu, Balboa Theatre-San Diego and many others.

Aerial Physique has been televised on the TODAY Show and Jill has been featured in People Magazine, Muscle and Fitness Magazine, Vogue, Shape and Latina Magazine. Additional articles and media coverage featuring Jill's work can be found in Prevention Magazine, Good Day LA, Inside Edition, Yahoo Celebrity, ABC 7 LA and many other media outlets. Jill is always excited to share her knowledge and expertise with you and help you live a life full of Beauty, Grace and Strength.

INTRODUCTION
Fit Principles

The Fit Principles will guide you in developing excellent workout habits that will assist you in gaining the results you want. It boils down to awareness and incorporating exercise into your daily life.

What is so important about core strength?
Core strength is the support system for your entire body. Without it, your body cannot function effectively and in time a weak core can lead to injury and possible health problems. In addition core strength helps to support your spine, helps you to look thinner and improves your overall workout performance. The 'core' is not only the 'six pack', it is a corset of power around your center, including 3 layers of abs. The glutes, hips and lower back muscles are also incorporated.

It's mind-body time … put down your cell phone!
The only way to achieve your desired results is through 100% focus, positive thinking and a solid mind-body connection. It's about being in the 'zone'. When you're working out it's YOU time, do your best to avoid all distractions and negative thoughts. Instead, focus on your breath and the task at hand.

What about your posture?
Standing properly offsets the perpetual force of gravity on the body, lessening stress on the spine and ensuring the joints work efficiently. Your muscles help to maintain your skeletal frame throughout your daily activities. Poor posture places additional force on your entire skeletal and internal system which can lead to an array of potential health issues including back & knee pain, headaches and neck & shoulder tension, just to name a few. The exercises within the following pages along with consistent stretching can help to correct imbalances and restore your ideal posture.

INTRODUCTION
Fit Principles

How many reps should I do?
Repetitions are the amount of times you repeat a specific movement or pattern. For most of the exercises in this book the suggested amount of reps is 10. As your strength and ability increases you may want to do 2-3 sets of 10 for optimal results. Listen to your body, avoid pushing to the point of strain and over exertion.

Get long and lean muscles using full range of motion!
For optimal results and benefits it's necessary to work each muscle through its full range of motion. It is important to keep tension in the muscle during each movement and not relaxing the part of the body being worked when lowering or releasing. Also be cautious not to hyperextend the joints (knees & elbows) at the end of your range of motion. Over time, this causes wear and tear on the joints and ligaments and does not lead to stronger muscles.

How often should you work out?
For best results commit to working out 3-5 days per week for 30-45 minutes at a time. If your schedule allows to workout every day, excellent! The length of your workout will vary according to how many exercises and sets you choose.
Keep in mind, *longer* workouts are not always *better* workouts.

INTRODUCTION
Pilates Concepts

Pilates History

Pilates (aka *'Contrology'* the art of control) utilizes the muscles of the core, abdominals, hips, glutes, inner thighs. They are often referred to as the "Powerhouse." The combination of strength, stretch and control are key factors when executing the movements outlined in this book. German born Joseph Pilates (1880-1967) was the originator of *'Pilates'* his system was developed in the early 1920s for the purpose of rehabilitation. Some of the first people treated by Pilates were soldiers returning from war and famous dancers such as Martha Graham and George Balanchine. Pilates is currently a popular physical fitness system.

Pilates Positioning Concepts

The Pilates concepts are key factors to remember while performing the exercises in this book. They will help lengthen, strengthen and tone your body and help keep you stable and injury free!

Using the "Powerhouse": The powerhouse refers to an area of your body which begins from the bottom of your ribs all the way to your hip line. It includes the abdominal muscles, low back muscles, pelvic floor, muscles around the hips, and the glutes. Powerhouse muscles work together to form a supportive corset for your trunk. They stabilize and they give aerial moves their dynamic strength. Joseph Pilates emphasized this area of the body in the program of training he designed. All Pilates movements originate from the powerhouse.

Scooping Abs In & Up: In Pilates we don't want to allow the tummy to pooch out nor do we want to suck in so much that we can't breathe. Instead, think of your abs drawing in towards your spine throughout every exercise. If we allow the abs to pooch out or press away when working out, our precision based movements will not be done correctly.

INTRODUCTION
Pilates Concepts

Pull Front Ribs Together: When scooping your abs in and up do not allow your front ribs to pop out. This postural practice can be a challenge. It involves relaxing the front ribs down and together to better recruit and engage the abdominals. It also helps to lengthen the spine and assists with correct alignment.

Tucking Under Versus Lengthening: One goal of Pilates is to lengthen your muscles as you strengthen them. When you are performing an exercise that instructs you to squeeze your glutes for example, it is not meant to shorten your spine or encourage you to tuck under. Instead, keep the length in your spine while engaging the surrounding muscles. You want to feel the back of your pelvis and the base of your spine on the mat.

Stabilize Using Pilates Stance: The Pilates Stance or Pilates V is a slight external rotating of the legs. A small V shape (not extreme dancer turn-out) encourages the use of the inner/outer thighs, hips and glutes and not the quadriceps (front of the thighs). Your heels are glued together and your knees remain soft (not locked or hyperextended). If the legs are parallel, usually the quads do all of the work and it's more challenging to connect to the powerhouse.

Spinal Articulation: Articulation of the spine involves moving one vertebra at a time. it is a foundational movement in Pilates. It wakes up the core and develops awareness to the connection between the abdominals and the spine.

Oppositional Reaching: Reaching one body part as far as possible from the other develops length. This helps to align and center the body with an added result of beautiful lines.

INTRODUCTION
Pilates Concepts

Control Without Tension: This can be a challenging concept for some to apply while moving. The focus is to find the happy medium of challenging yourself but not to the point that you tense up. This is where fluidity of movement and grace is developed. Remember to breath, inhale at the start of a movement and exhale at its completion. Also, don't push yourself beyond your point of control. Think about the grace and ease of movement that dancers possess, it all begins in your mind!

Lengthening the Neck: It's very common in Pilates to tense up around your shoulders and neck. Here's a helpful note, think about lengthening the back of your neck and dropping your chin slightly down, towards your chest. You want your neck to follow the line of your spine. In today's world of smart phone and computer use, most of the populations head is too far forward! This causes neck pain, headaches and tight upper backs/shoulders. Pilates movements can help remedy this issue!

"The mind, when housed within a healthful body, possesses a glorious sense of power." -Joseph Pilates

INTRODUCTION
Stretching Methods

When it comes to overall peak performance, **stretching** is considered among the top protocols for professional aerialists and athletes. It's also vital in preventing injuries even for those who perform rigorous workouts in the gym **and** for the general public with an active lifestyle. There are four key methods of stretching, Static, Dynamic, Passive, Active. When each stretch is administered correctly, they can help facilitate a more functional, more flexible body.

Static Stretching
Static means having no motion, being at rest. This stretch technique is a position held still, for a certain amount of time, ranging from 10 to 30 seconds. It is the most common form of stretching and is safe and effective for improving flexibility in the vast majority of those seeking additional mobility and movement.

Dynamic Stretching
This stretch technique is more involved and requires movement through logical positions coupled with numerous and repetitive maneuvers. Ten to fifteen movements are common and is favored by today's top athletes. The Pilates exercises in this book incorporate dynamic stretching.

Passive Stretching
Using a towel, band, strap or other device to aid in flexibility is key to this form of stretching. The body part is relaxed while the device or person is assisting with this stretch. Make sure to pay attention to the force being used, as injury can occur if pushed beyond flexibility boundaries.

Active Stretching
No apparatus or equipment needed here. Use your own strength and muscles and not an external force to move the body into a comfortable stretching position. This is a low risk, yet effective form of gaining additional flexibility. With active stretching, you relax the muscle you're trying to stretch and rely on the opposing muscle to initiate the stretch.

INTRODUCTION
Anatomy & Muscles

Pictured below are the main muscles at work during aerial practice and the exercises in this guide.

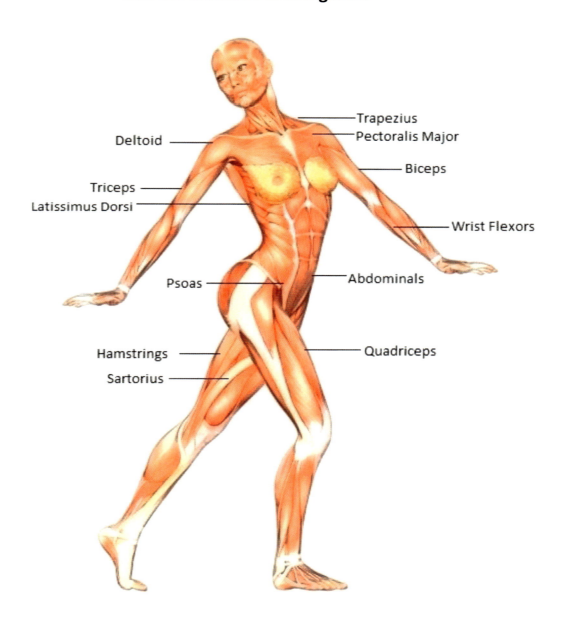

INTRODUCTION
Anatomy & Muscles

Abdominals: There are four muscles that make up the abdominal wall. All support the core but each functions differently. **Transverse**, the deepest of the four assists in stabilizing the spine and forcing air out of the lungs. The **internal and external obliques** assist in rotating, flexing and side bending movements. Lastly the **rectus,** also known as the 'six pack', works to flex (bend) the trunk.

Biceps: The front of the upper arm, it bends and supinates (turns palm upwards) the forearm. It is active during chin-ups.

Deltoid: A shoulder muscle that assists in lifting the arm away from the body.

Hamstrings: A group of three muscles in the back of the leg that bend the knee and extend (straighten) the thigh. When flexible, this muscle group helps achieve a pike position.

Latissimi Dorsi: Meaning 'Widest Back Muscle' it is your climbing and pull-up muscle. Also known as the 'lats', they are your wings during upper body movements and aerial work.

Pectoralis Major: They are your main chest muscle, at work when doing push-ups.

Psoas: Deep hip flexor muscle that flexes the thigh and turns out the leg.

Quadriceps: The front of your thigh. A group of four muscles that assist in straightening the knee and flexing the thigh.

Sartorius: The inner thigh. It is the longest muscle in the body. Turns out the hips. When flexible, it aids in achieving a straddle position.

Trapezius: Upper, middle and lower traps work to move the shoulder blades up and down. They also work when holding the arm to the side or overhead.

Triceps: The back of the upper arm, it extends (straightens) the forearm. At work in many aerial feats.

Wrist Flexors: The forearm. Bends wrists towards the body.

INTRODUCTION
Equipment Needed

Yoga/Exercise Mat: Mats come in many thicknesses and colors. Choose a mat that is comfortable for you and supportive on your spine.

Pull-Up Bar: If you plan to workout at home get a pull-up bar that you can install in your doorway. Be sure it is secure before each use. Alternate options are monkey bars or a gym.

Free Weights: These hand held weights are commonly used in many fitness programs. For exercises in this book 2lb-5lb weights are recommended.

2 Yoga Blocks: Yoga blocks are most commonly made of foam and are about the size of a brick. They are a prop used to raise the floor to your hands, deepen stretches and help maintain proper alignment.

Stability Ball: These large balls generally come in sizes ranging from 45-75cm. The size to choose varies with your height. The ideal size for you would equal a 90 degree angle with your legs when sitting upright on the ball, with feet flat on the floor.

Yoga Strap or Stretch Band: Yoga straps are usually made of cotton. Stretch bands are most commonly made of latex and used for resistance and stretching. Both will work to help deepen your stretching practice.

Body Band: These large circular bands come in different resistance levels. They have many functions but for the purpose of this book it is used to loop over the pull-up bar to assist with achieving pull-ups and chin-ups.

Ankle Weights - Optional: These are adjustable weights that strap around the ankle and are usually 3-5lbs. They are used to increase the intensity of exercises in this book.

INTRODUCTION
Test Your Fitness Level

Test your current fitness level with the 4 exercises pictured below. They will assess your muscular endurance and flexibility within each of the sections in this guide. Be sure to warm up with a brisk walk or light cardio. Take note of your assessment and repeat the same test every 30 days and chart your progress!

CORE TEST
Hollow Body Hold - Page 17
How long can you hold hollow body in proper alignment with your lower back on the mat and toes in line with your nose?
GOAL - 60 Second Hold

LOWER BODY/CORE TEST
Pike Press Up - Page 43
How long can you hold your lower body off the mat with straight legs?

GOAL - 30 Second Hold

INTRODUCTION
Test Your Fitness Level

UPPER BODY TEST
Chin-Up Hold - Page 118
How long can you hold your chin above the bar with your elbows in towards your hips and torso in hollow body?

GOAL - 60 Second Hold

FLEXIBILITY TEST
Front Splits - Page 138
How low can you get in the splits with square hips?

GOAL - All the way down!

INTRODUCTION
How to Use This Book

This book was created as a tool to help you achieve the strength of a cirque performer, the legs of a ballet dancer and the abs of a Pilates pro. With consistency, focus and passion you can achieve the results you desire! The exercises in this guide are not meant to do all at once. It's best to choose 6-8 from each of the Core, Lower Body & Upper Body sections that work the major muscle groups followed by 10-15 minutes of stretching for a well-rounded workout. In each exercise focus on your abs pulling in and up, work through your full range of motion and lengthen, lengthen, lengthen!

If you are working with an injury or are pregnant there are many exercises that may need to be modified further or completely avoided. It is recommended to consult with your doctor prior to beginning a new fitness regimen. If you have a lower back injury or disc issue, it is best to avoid flexion of the spine. In most cases flexion (forward bending) worsens the condition. Instead, keep your spine long and do exercises that encourage extension (cobra for example). Although uncomfortable at times, no exercise should ever hurt. Your body is the only one you get, preserve it, nurture it and be grateful for everything it can do!

TRAINING GUIDELINES

- Never push to the point of pain
- Be mindful of your posture and alignment
- Your core rules! Keep your abs pulled in and up during each exercise
- Continue to challenge yourself by adding more reps, weight or longer holds
- Be sure you are warmed up prior to stretching
- Stay present by focusing on your breath and the exercise at hand
- Set goals and track your progress!

CORE PROGRAM

Achieving strong, flat and toned abs is not just about doing sit ups, it's about learning how to properly recruit your core body muscles. Your core includes your abdominals, lower back, glutes and surrounding muscles which support your spine. The more in-tune you are with your core, the more beneficial each exercise is. Eventually, it will lead to a corset of muscles that support you at all times.

CORE PROGRAM
Hollow Body Position

1. Begin lying on your back with your knees bent and feet on the mat. Reach your arms long by your sides.

2. Draw your abs in to lift your knees up to table top position (hips & knees at right angles) while curling your chin up and over your chest to lift your shoulders off the floor.

3. Extend your legs out long in front of you while keeping your shoulders lifted. Reach your arms to your sides.

4. For an added challenge, reach your arms back by your ears. Hold for 30-60 seconds.

CORE PROGRAM
Hollow Body Position

WHY?
The Hollow Body Position is a fundamental position in this book along with aerial and gymnastics. It's one of the most important positions to master, as it's the base of many of the exercises to come.

TECHNIQUE TIPS & MODIFICATIONS

- When lifting your head and shoulders up in step 2 think about curling your chin up and over your chest so the weight of your head is far enough forward that your abs can support you and you're not straining your neck.
- Press your lower back into the floor as you scoop your abs in and up.
- If you feel you are not able to lower your legs as pictured in step 3 straighten them up to the ceiling instead. As you build strength in your core gradually work on lowering them down. The eventual goal is toes in line with your nose.
- Slightly turn-out your legs when they are extended to disengage the quadriceps and allow your inner thighs and glutes to work. Squeeze your inner thighs and glutes tightly the entire time.
- Point your feet and reach your legs long in front of you.
- When reaching your arms by your ears in step 4, do not allow your shoulders to sink to the mat.
- Don't forget to breathe!
- Begin holding for as long as you can, and maintain your form, eventually working up to a 60 second hold.

CORE PROGRAM
Plank Position

Plank Place your hands palms down underneath your shoulders. Pull your navel in towards your spine to lengthen your lower back. Squeeze the back of your legs together and firm the front of your thighs.

Side Plank From your plank position place one hand on your hip and roll to the outside edges of your feet. Your supporting arm is strong with your hand on the mat underneath your shoulder.

Forearm Plank Place your forearms down with your elbows underneath your shoulders and interlace your fingers. Pull your navel in towards your spine to lengthen your lower back. Squeeze the back of your legs together and firm the front of your thighs.

Side Forearm Plank Lie on your side with your legs straight and stacked on top of one another. Place your forearm on the floor with your elbow under your shoulder. Activate your core and lift your hips up. Draw your supporting shoulder down away from your ear.

CORE PROGRAM
Plank Position

WHY?

The Plank, Side Plank, Forearm Plank and Side Forearm Plank work your abs, shoulders and muscles in your back. All are foundation positions that are important for overall strength and stability of your body.

TECHNIQUE TIPS & MODIFICATIONS

- Avoid sinking in your shoulder blades. Instead, maintain lift in your trunk as you press away from the floor with your hands or forearms.
- Hold each position for 30-60 seconds.
- In some cases a slight tuck under of the pelvis is necessary to avoid arching the lower back. Think of drawing your tailbone down towards your heels to maintain length in your spine.
- Keep the back of your neck long and in alignment of the rest of your spine. Reach the top of your head forward not down towards the floor.
- Having your legs together allows you to squeeze your inner thighs and glutes and achieve a more connected position.
- If you feel the plank in your wrists, think about pushing away from the floor with the heels of your hands, this will help take pressure off your wrists. If you still feel discomfort, try stretching your wrists prior to this exercise.
- Option to do the exercise pictured below during Side Plank and Side Forearm Plank - move your hips a few inches up and down for an added oblique workout. Be sure to lift from your waist on each lift, no sinking into your bottom shoulder!

CORE PROGRAM
Pilates 100s

1. Begin lying on your back with your knees bent and arms long by your sides.

2. Pull your abs in to lift your knees up to table top position (hips and knees at right angles) while curling your chin up and over your chest to lift your shoulders off the floor.

3. Straighten your legs up. Squeeze your inner thighs together and tighten your glutes. Pump your arms up and down with a small range of motion, keeping your elbows straight. Inhale for five arm pumps and exhale for five pumps. Repeat the cycle ten times for a total of 100 pumps.

4. For an added abdominal challenge lower your legs down as low as you can with your lower back rooted to the floor while maintaining the engagement of your abs (no pooching abs allowed). End by hugging your knees into your chest and relaxing your head down to the mat.

CORE PROGRAM
Pilates 100s

WHY?
The Pilates 100s is a breathing and abdominal exercise meant to warm up the body for the following exercises. The goal of the exercise is to have your toes at eye level while maintaining a flat back on the floor.

TECHNIQUE TIPS & MODIFICATIONS
- If you have a sensitive lower back squeezing your glutes and the backs of your upper inner thighs will help to support it.
- If you are feeling it more in your lower back place your legs in table top until you increase the strength in your abs. Be mindful that you are drawing your abs in and up and not allowing them to protrude with each breath.
- If your neck bothers you rest your head down and lift again when you are ready. Neck pain in abdominal exercises is usually from lifting from the neck itself. Instead think of curling your chin up and over your neck so your abs can support the weight of your head.
- The arm pumps originate from the lattimus dorsi and not the shoulders or neck. Think of stretching your fingertips past your tush and maintain a stable trunk as you pump your arms.

Use for students who struggle w/ X-back or inversions

CORE PROGRAM
Roll Ups

1. Lie on your back with legs straight and feet gently pointed. Reach your arms back as far as possible keeping your front ribs pulling together.

2. Squeeze your glutes and the backs of your inner thighs together. Begin to reach your arms in front of you.

3. Curl your chin up and over your chest and lift your shoulders off the floor while keeping your lower back rooted down.

4. Continue to roll up feeling the articulation of your spine as it leaves the mat. Reach your fingertips forward as you pull your navel into your spine.

5. Begin rolling down focusing on retracing your path.

6. End on your back with arms reaching up & back. Repeat 5-10x.

CORE PROGRAM
Roll Ups

WHY?
The Roll Up is an articulation exercise that stretches and strengthens the spine. When done correctly it works your deep abdominals and improves flexibility.

TECHNIQUE TIPS & MODIFICATIONS

- It's common for the legs to lift when rolling up and down due to the hip flexors taking over for the abs. To avoid this, squeeze the backs of your upper inner thighs together to maintain stillness of your lower body.
- When beginning the roll up, bring your chin towards your chest to ensure your abs do the work to lift your torso up & you don't pull from your neck.
- Focus on articulating through the spine when rolling up and down. Do not depend on momentum of throwing your arms forward to lift you up.
- This exercise is not about trying to touch your toes. Instead, use the oppositional reach of pulling your belly button deep in towards your spine as you stretch forward. This creates a nice stretch for your spine while improving your abdominal strength.

INADEQUATE ABDOMINAL STABILIZATION

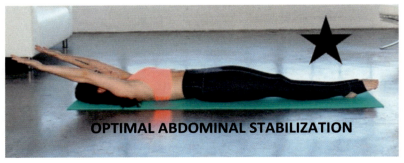

OPTIMAL ABDOMINAL STABILIZATION

CORE PROGRAM
Roll Over

1. Lie on your back with legs straight up. Reach your arms long by your sides for stability.

2. Lower your legs until they are at a 60 degree angle from the mat. Squeeze the backs of your upper inner thighs together.

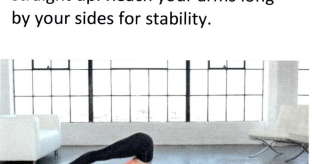

3. Using your "powerhouse" lift your legs up and overhead. Open your legs hip distance apart and flex your feet. Make sure your weight is on your upper back in between your shoulders and not on your neck.

4. Keeping your feet flexed and legs hip distance apart, slowly lower yourself back to the mat while articulating through your spine.

5. End with your back flat and legs up. Repeat the same sequence, starting with legs apart as you roll over and rolling down with legs together. Repeat 3-6x.

CORE PROGRAM
Straddle Roll Over

1. Lie on your back with legs straight up. Reach your arms long by your sides for stability.

2. Open your legs wide into a wide straddle. Legs are straight & turned out with pointed feet.

3. Using you "powerhouse" lift your legs up and overhead maintaining your wide straddle.

4. Lower your torso to the mat while articulating through your spine.

5. Arrive in a straddle with your lower abs scooped in and back flat on the floor.

6. Close your legs together at a 60 degree angle from the floor. Repeat 3-6x.

CORE PROGRAM
Roll Over & Straddle Roll Over

WHY?

The Roll Over stretches and articulates the spine by using the core muscles. It's an excellent exercise for improving your inversions, especially for aerialists.

TECHNIQUE TIPS & MODIFICATIONS

- Make sure you are warmed up before attempting this move.
- If you cannot perform the roll over without bending your knees or supporting your lower back with your hands to get you over, then you are not strong enough to do the exercise or you have a very tight lower back and/or hamstrings. Work on roll ups, rolling like a ball and the ab series of 5 in the pages that follow until you feel your ability improve.
- Help stabilize your torso while lifting your legs overhead by pressing weight into the palms of your hands. Once inverted, reach out long through your fingertips.
- Pull into your abdominals and initiate the movement from the back of your hips do not allow your legs to swing you over.
- When you are in the full roll over (step 3) keep the back of your neck lengthened and DO NOT turn your head to the side, doing so may result in injury.
- For an added hamstring stretch, focus on firmly flexing your feet during steps 4-5 of the Roll Over.
- If you are an aerialist wanting to improve your inversions, the Straddle Roll Over is very beneficial.

CORE PROGRAM
Rolling Like a Ball

1. Begin seated with your knees open slightly and drawn close to your chest. Place your hands on the front of your shins with your elbows out to the sides. Scoop your low abs in and hover your feet above the mat. Gently drop your chin towards your chest to complete the shape of a ball.

2. Initiate rolling back by drawing your belly button so deep into your spine it knocks you off balance, continue to roll to your upper back. Maintain your ball shape as you roll back up to step 1. Repeat 5-10x.

WHY?
Rolling Like a Ball is a great exercise to improve balance while working the abdominals and massaging the spine.

TECHNIQUE TIPS & MODIFICATIONS

- Initiate the movement by drawing your abs in and up, to roll up think of your abs as your "brakes" to stop you at the top.
- Do not allow your heels to fly away from your tush to help you up, maintain a firm tuck or ball shape the entire time.
- Keep your neck long and shoulders down and away from your ears.
- Be careful not to roll back too far on your neck, stop when you are on your upper back in between your shoulder blades.
- For an added abdominal challenge place your elbows on top of your knees, keep your elbows and knees connected as you roll.

CORE PROGRAM
Single Leg Stretch - Ab Series of Five

1. Begin seated with your knees bent, feet flat on the floor, spine lengthened and arms reaching forward.

2. Draw your abs in and up, roll your torso down to the mat, stop when the tips of your shoulders are hovering above the floor. Draw your chin towards your chest and look towards your tummy.

5. Pull your right knee into your chest, place your outside hand on your ankle and your inside hand just below your knee. Lift your left leg up until your abs feel challenged, yet still keep your back flat on the floor.

4. Switch legs. Make sure you place your outside hand close to your ankle and inside hand just below your knee. This helps to keep your legs in proper anatomical alignment.
Repeat 10x.

CORE PROGRAM
Single Leg Stretch - Ab Series of Five

WHY?

The Single Leg Stretch is the first of five exercises referred to as the *Ab Series of Five.* All five exercises can be done individually while building strength and are meant to flow from one to the next. The goal of each exercise is to stay completely still in your torso as your legs and arms move in different directions to work your core. This exercise stretches your hips while working your core.

TECHNIQUE TIPS & MODIFICATIONS

- Pull the bent leg close into your chest while reaching the straight leg away from you creating an oppositional two way stretch.
- Do your best to keep your outside hand on your ankle and your inside hand just below your knee, this helps to keep your legs properly aligned throughout the exercise.
- The straight leg should not go below hip level. Maintain a position that allows you to keep your abdominals working and lower back flat.
- Inhale to begin and exhale to switch legs, deep breathing allows for deep abdominal work.
- For a sensitive lower back, extend the opposite straight leg to the ceiling.

CORE PROGRAM
Double Leg Stretch - Ab Series of Five

1. Lie on your back with your head and shoulders lifted. Both knees are bent into your chest with your hands on your shins and elbows wide.

2. Reach your arms back by your ears and your legs long in front of you at a 45 degree angle from the floor.

3. Draw your abdominals in as you hug your knees into your chest, simultaneously circle your arms to the side and meet your hands back on top of your shins. Repeat 5-10x.

CORE PROGRAM
Double Leg Stretch - Ab Series of Five

WHY?
The Double Leg Stretch is the second of five exercises referred to as the *Ab Series of Five.* This exercise lengthens your body while strengthening your core.

TECHNIQUE TIPS & MODIFICATIONS
- Support your neck by curling your chin up and over your chest the entire time. Think of brining the weight of your head far enough forward that your abs can support the weight of your head and you're not relying on your neck.
- Keep your shoulders and head lifted off the floor as you reach your arms back by your ears.
- Squeeze your glutes and your upper inner thighs together when extending your legs, this helps to support your lower back.
- Keep your center rooted to the floor throughout each repetition.
- For a sensitive lower back extend your legs up towards the ceiling instead of at a 45 degree angle.

CORE PROGRAM
Single Straight Leg Stretch - Ab Series of Five

1. Lie on your back with your head and shoulders lifted. Extend your right leg up, grab your ankle with both hands. Lift your left leg up to a height at which your lower back can continue to press into the mat. Pull your abs in deeper while pulling the top leg closer to you with two gentle pulses, simultaneously take two percussive inhales.

2. Scissor the legs and switch. Pull the left leg closer to you with two gentle pulses, simultaneously take two percussive exhales. Repeat 10x.

CORE PROGRAM
Single Straight Leg Stretch - Ab Series of Five

WHY?
The Single Straight Leg Stretch is the third of five exercises referred to as the *Ab Series of Five*. This exercise in particular, is excellent for stretching and elongating the back of the legs (hamstrings).

TECHNIQUE TIPS & MODIFICATIONS
- Keep your gaze at your tummy, make sure it is behaving and staying scooped in and up at all times!
- If it is too difficult to reach your ankle, hold around your calf muscle or behind your thigh instead. Never grab behind the back of your knee.
- Maintain completely straight legs and gently pointed feet the entire time, think about reaching long all the way out through your toes.
- Pay attention to your shoulders, make sure they are not hunching while pulsing your leg in.
- For an added abdominal challenge, try the exercise with your arms reaching long by your sides.

INADEQUATE LEG ENGAGEMENT

CORE PROGRAM
Double Straight Leg Stretch - Ab Series of Five

1. Lie on your back with your hands behind your head, one on top of the other. Lift your head and shoulders up and extend your legs straight to the ceiling in Pilates stance.

2. Squeeze your glutes and the backs of your upper thighs together. Scoop your abs in and up while you anchor your lower back to the mat. Lower your legs to a 45 degree angle. Lift your chest towards your legs as you return to the starting position. Repeat 10x.

Modification

For a sensitive lower back or if you cannot keep you lower back to the mat while doing this exercise, try the following modification. Begin with your legs in a diamond shape with soft knees. Lower your legs as much as you can, keeping your back to the mat and abdominals scooped. Lift up to your starting position. Repeat 10x.

CORE PROGRAM
Double Straight Leg Stretch - Ab Series of Five

WHY?

The Double Straight Leg Stretch is the fourth of five exercises referred to as the *Ab Series of Five*. The intensity of this exercise is felt in the upper and lower abs. Use modifications as you see fit.

TECHNIQUE TIPS & MODIFICATIONS

- Do not allow your lower back to arch as you lower your legs.
- To avoid neck pain, think about lifting from your abs and the back of your shoulders, not the neck itself.
- Keep your elbows wide and shoulders drawing away from your ears.
- Lift your chest towards your thighs on each repetition.
- Maintain a tight tush and squeeze your inner thighs the entire time.
- For an added challenge, perform the exercise with ankle weights to increase the intensity. This is great for aerialists who want to improve their core strength and power while in the air!

CORE PROGRAM
Criss-Cross - Ab Series of Five

1. Lie on your back with your hands behind your head, chest lifted and legs in table top position.

2. Extend your left leg long in front of you and twist your torso to the right. Perform the twist from your waist and not from your neck or shoulders.

3. Optional For an added core challenge, extend your right leg long in front of you to meet your left leg before twisting to the left.

4. Keep your center firmly grounded to the mat as you switch sides and twist to the left. Repeat 10x.

CORE PROGRAM
Criss-Cross - Ab Series of Five

WHY?

The Criss-Cross is the last of five exercises referred to as the *Ab Series of Five*. This exercise works your external obliques while slimming your waistline.

TECHNIQUE TIPS & MODIFICATIONS

- Do not allow your body to rock side to side while twisting, instead focus on keeping your lower back glued to the mat and twist from your waist.
- Keep your elbows wide and look toward your back elbow on each repetition to help increase your range of motion.
- Think about aiming your opposite armpit toward your knee, not your elbow to your knee.
- Don't allow your outstretched leg to drop so low that you lower back in no longer anchored to the mat.
- For added intensity, meet both legs together out in front of you before twisting to the opposite side (step 3).
- Inhale as you pass through the center and exhale deeply on each twist.

CORE PROGRAM
Superman - Back Extension

1. Lie on your stomach. Begin with your forehead touching the floor, arms reaching forward and legs open hip distance apart. Pull your abs in and up as you lift your chest off the floor keeping your legs down. Lower your chest with control. Repeat 10x.

2. Perform the same steps as in step 1. This time, allow your legs to lift up with you. Lower down with control. Repeat 10x.

WHY?

Superman strengthens the muscles along your spine, in particular erector spinae. It's important your back muscles are strong to add additional support for your overall structure and posture (remember your core is not only your abs!). In this exercise focus on the front and back of your body working together.

TECHNIQUE TIPS & MODIFICATIONS

- Pull your abs in and up away from the floor with each lift to maintain length in your lower back.
- Keep the back of your neck long, gaze down instead of forward.
- Feel as though you are stretching in opposition, fingers and toes reaching as far apart as possible.

CORE PROGRAM
V-Ups #1

1. Begin balancing on your tailbone in a seated table top position with your abs scooped in arms reaching forward. Legs are together and feet are gently pointed.

2. Articulate through your spine as you lower your torso to the mat while simultaneously extending your legs long in front of you. Stop when the tips of your shoulders are hovering above the mat and your legs are at a height that you can control.

3. Pull into your center, with control, float your legs and torso up to your starting table top position. Repeat 10x.

"Physical fitness can neither be achieved by wishful thinking nor outright purchase." -Joseph Pilates

CORE PROGRAM
V-Ups #2

1. Begin from hollow body position with your arms reaching back. Inner thighs and glutes are squeezing firmly together.

2. Draw your abs in and begin to reach your arms forward. Slowly peel your spine off the mat until you arrive in a V shape balancing on your tailbone.

3. Scoop your low abs in to initiate lowering your torso and legs. Articulate through your spine on your way down.

4. Arrive in your hollow body position with arms and legs reaching in opposition. Repeat 10x.

CORE PROGRAM
V-Ups #1 & #2

WHY?

The V-Up is an excellent all-encompassing core workout which proves to be a challenge for all fitness levels. It's a great exercise to help chart your progress in both strength and flexibility.

TECHNIQUE TIPS & MODIFICATIONS

- Do not lower your legs past your point of control. Doing so will result in ineffective movement and possibly pain or discomfort in your lower back.
- Begin with V-Up #1 only, as your strength increases work up to V-Up #2.
- Do not swing your arms forward to help you lift your torso up, instead reach your arms forward and pull into your center on each repetition.
- Do not allow your lower back to arch when arriving at the top of your V-Up, slightly curl your tailbone underneath, to ensure you are working from your center and not using your lower back.
- Squeezing your inner thighs and glutes will help to support & stabilize you.
- If you are injury free and can successfully perform V-Up #2 with your lower back firmly on the floor, try it with ankle weights for an added challenge
- Have a little fun with it! Try this sequence pictured below:
  Table Top - Straight Leg V - Hollow body - Table Top - Repeat

CORE PROGRAM
Pike Press-Up

1. Begin seated with legs forward in a pike. Place yoga blocks to the side of you as pictured. Place your hands on top of the blocks with your fingers facing forward.

2. Press weight into your hands and lift your tush off the mat. Elongate your neck as you draw your shoulders away from your ears. Repeat this step until you feel strong enough in your upper body, core and thighs to attempt step 3.

3. Press weight into your hands while simultaneously lifting your entire lower body off the mat. Keep your legs straight and firmly squeezing together. Hold for 10-30 seconds.

CORE PROGRAM
Pike Press-Up

WHY?
The Pike Press-Up is a challenge for the core muscles, the front of the thighs and the upper body. This is a great drill if you want to increase your strength and awareness for handstands.

TECHNIQUE TIPS & MODIFICATIONS

- Opposition is key, press down into the blocks as you reach the top of your head upwards.
- Scoop your lower abs in to avoid arching your lower back.
- It requires a lot of strength to perform step 3. Work your way up to it gradually.
- Your legs must be absolutely straight in order to achieve the full benefits of this exercise. Engage your quadriceps and squeeze your inner thighs together.
- Don't forget about your feet! Keep your feet pointed throughout.
- Breathe ... this is a tough one.
- If you are having a hard time lifting your legs, work on the Pike Lifts on the next page.
- Once you feel confident doing the exercise with the blocks, try it without! The blocks raise the floor up to you which makes this exercise easier to learn.

CORE PROGRAM
Pike Lifts

1. Begin seated with your legs out in front of you in a pike position. Place your hands on either side of your knees with your palms flat. Scoop your abs in deeply.

2. Press your hands down firmly into the mat as you lift your legs up. Be sure to keep both legs absolutely straight and pressing together. Lower down with control. Repeat 10X.

"It does not matter how slowly you go as long as you do not stop." -*Confucius*

CORE PROGRAM
Single Leg Lifts & Straddle Lifts

Single Leg Lifts

1. Begin seated with your legs in a straddle. Turn your torso to the side and place your hands on either side of your knee. Root your palms down into the floor as you draw your abs in and up.

2. Lift your leg as high as you can keeping it straight. Lower with control. Repeat 10x. Switch legs.

Straddle Lifts

1. Begin seated with your legs in a straddle. Place your hands in front of you with your fingers facing forward.

2. Press into your hands as you lift your legs up as high as you can keeping them straight and turned out. Repeat 10x.

CORE PROGRAM
Pike Lifts, Single Leg Lifts & Straddle Lifts

WHY?

Pike Lifts, Single Leg Lifts and Straddle Lifts work not only your core but also your hip flexors and the front of your thighs. If you are an aerialist, all three are excellent exercises to help better your straight leg inversions and strength in the air.

TECHNIQUE TIPS & MODIFICATIONS

- If it is too challenging to have your hands next to your knees on the Pike Lifts and Single Leg Lifts bring them closer to you. The further forward the hands, the harder this exercise is.
- Do your best to keep your palms flat as you lift your legs up.
- Think 'tight is light' the tighter you engage the muscles in your legs, the lighter they become.
- Keep your feet pointed the entire time, it finishes the line in your legs and also helps you to properly engage them.
- Scoop your abs in and up to imitate each lift.
- For an extra challenge add ankle weights.

CORE PROGRAM
Hand-Stand Prep - Ball Tuck

1. Begin in a plank position with your shins and tops of your feet on the ball. Align your shoulders over your wrists. Pull your abs in and up while drawing your tailbone down.

2. Bend your knees into your chest while maintaining the alignment of your shoulders over your wrists. Extend your legs back to step 1. Repeat 10x.

"True success is overcoming the fear of being unsuccessful."
-*Paul Sweeney*

CORE PROGRAM
Hand-Stand Prep - Ball Pike

1. Begin in a plank position with your shins and tops of your feet on the ball. Align your shoulders over your wrists. Pull your abs in and up while drawing your tailbone down.

2. Keep your legs straight as you pike your hips up. Continue to lift until your hips are above your shoulders. Lower back to your plank with control. Repeat 10x.

"The greater the obstacle, the more glory in overcoming it."
-Moliere

CORE PROGRAM
Hand-Stand Prep - Ball Tucks & Pikes

WHY?

The Ball Tuck and Ball Pike use mainly your abdominals and shoulders. They are both wonderful preparation exercises for hand-stands. Proper alignment is key to achieving results and avoiding injury.

TECHNIQUE TIPS & MODIFICATIONS

- Before giving these a try make sure you have a solid plank and hollow body position you can hold for at least 60 seconds.
- To get on the ball lay over it with the front of your torso, walk your hands out until you reach a plank position.
- Alignment is vital, align your wrists underneath your shoulders during each rep.
- Balancing on the ball can be tricky, make sure your ball is fully inflated and enough of your lower leg is on the ball to support you.
- The Pike position requires a lot of strength in your shoulders in order to support your elevated hips. Practice plank by itself along with the weight lifting exercises in the pages to come.
- Initiate each rep by pulling into your center.
- Press away from the floor with your hands to avoid sinking in your upper back and winging your shoulder blades.

CORE PROGRAM
Wall Hand-Stand - Pike

1. Sit with your back against the wall and your legs straight out in front of you forming an L shape.

2. Stand where your ankles were in step 1.

3. Fold forward and Place your hands shoulder distance apart on the mat just to the side of your feet.

4. Press away from the floor and place one leg behind you on the wall.

5. Join your other leg to meet it as you align your hips above your shoulders.

6. Extend one leg upwards. Lower it and lift the other leg. Repeat.

CORE PROGRAM
Wall Hand-Stand - Pike

WHY?

The Wall Hand-Stand Pike helps you to find your proper hand-stand alignment with the use of the wall. You'll also strengthen not only your core but your upper body and improve your balance as well!

TECHNIQUE TIPS & MODIFICATIONS

- Stretch and warm up your shoulders and wrists prior to hand-stands.
- Step 1 helps you to measure the proper distance from the wall for your hand-stand.
- You are forming a similar shape in step 1 and step 5, however in step 5 you're upside down!
- Lengthen your arms and make sure your elbows are straight, bent elbows do not serve as strong support for the rest of your body to balance.
- Press away from the floor as you lift your legs up onto the wall.
- Keep your neck long throughout.
- Once inverted don't forget to breathe!
- It's vital that your alignment is correct, the hips must be stacked over the shoulders.
- Do not let your extended leg in step 6 go behind you, doing so will make you arch your back. Instead, extend the leg slightly forward of your torso to ensure you maintain hollow body in your torso.
- To come down re-trace your path and carefully walk your legs down the wall.
- Option to hold step 5 for 30-60 seconds to strengthen your shoulders and core.

CORE PROGRAM
Wall Hand-Stand

1. Begin in a lunge position a couple feet away from the wall.

2. Place your hands down, shoulder distance apart and your fingers a few inches away from the wall.

3. Begin to transfer your weight forward into your hands as you bend your supporting leg and kick your other leg upward.

4. Continue to kick until one leg meets the wall. Extend your opposite leg up, keep one foot on the wall for balance.

5. Continue to press away from the floor, once you find your alignment, join both legs together and balance without touching the wall.

CORE PROGRAM
Wall Hand-Stand

WHY?
The Wall Hand-Stand prepares you for a free standing balance without the wall. Hand-stands are a true test of strength, mobility, alignment and balance.

TECHNIQUE TIPS & MODIFICATIONS
- Stretch and warm-up your shoulders and wrists prior to hand-stands.
- Keep your arms straight the entire time, loose arms will not support your body weight and may result in a fall.
- Commit to kicking up in steps 3-4, the wall is there to support you!
- Once you've kicked up, avoid placing both heels on the wall, this will make you arch your back and mis-align your hand-stand. Instead, place one foot on the wall (the leg that did the kicking) and extend the opposite leg straight up.
- Gaze in between your fingers, press away from the floor and stack your hips above your shoulders. Pull your abs in and up to ensure your lower back remains flat.
- When attempting to take both feet off the wall, the toes are slightly in front of your torso to ensure you remain in hollow body.
- When your feet leave the wall and you are attempting to balance squeeze your inner thighs and glutes tightly together, this will help stabilize you.
- When in your hand-stand use your finger tips to help you find your balance, when you are "balancing" you are actively pressing away from the floor and using your hands to help you maintain balance.
- Remain lifted and pulled into your center throughout, you will not balance without control of your center.

CORE PROGRAM
Vertical Abs - Hollow Body Hang

1. Begin hanging from a pull-up bar. Hands shoulder distance apart with fingers facing out. Legs pressing together and toes slightly forward of your shoulders.

2. Engage your abdominals and draw your ribcage together in the front. Lengthen your neck and draw your shoulders away from your ears. Hold for 30-60 seconds.

"Limitations live only in our mind. But if we use our imaginations, our possibilities become limitless."
-Jamie Paolinetti

CORE PROGRAM
Vertical Abs - Hollow Body Hang

WHY?
The Hollow Body Hang is a fundamental shape for the core exercises in the pages to come. It is also the base of your pull-ups and chin-ups. It's excellent for building core strength, grip strength along with strong yet mobile shoulders.

TECHNIQUE TIPS & MODIFICATIONS
- If necessary, stand on a chair to reach the pull-up bar.
- Pull your shoulders down away from your ears as you lengthen your neck while hanging.
- The hollow body hang is a fundamental position in gymnastics and aerial. It's crucial that your form is to the best of your ability before moving on to more challenging exercises.
- Don't forget to breathe throughout!
- Start with holding as long as you can, maintaining integrity in your form, eventually working up to 60 seconds.
- The same hollow body position done on the floor is duplicated from a hanging position.

CORE PROGRAM
Vertical Abs - Tuck

1. Begin from hollow body hang as described on page 55.

2. Maintain stillness in your upper body as you tuck your knees up towards your chest. Extend your legs down with control.

Optional Oblique Tucks

Begin from your hollow body hang position. Tuck and aim your knees to one side, targeting your obliques. Lower back to hollow body and repeat to the other side. Option to hold your knees in a tuck and lift them from side to side.

CORE PROGRAM
Vertical Abs - Tuck

WHY?
The Hanging Tuck is an excellent core and hip flexor strengthening exercise. Adding a twist targets the obliques which helps develop your internal 'corset' and slim the waistline.

TECHNIQUE TIPS & MODIFICATIONS

- If necessary, stand on a chair to reach the pull-up bar.
- If you find yourself swinging while doing this exercise think about using your abs to lift the weight of your legs up rather than using momentum to perform the lift.
- Keep your legs together and feet gently pointed the entire time.
- Don't forget to breathe! Inhale to tuck, exhale to lower.
- Repeat 10x eventually working your way up to 2-3 sets of 10.
- Pay close attention that your shoulders don't shrug by your ears. Draw your shoulders down your back as you lengthen your neck.
- Your grip will get a workout too!
- Once you can perform the exercise with excellent form and control, option to add ankle weights as pictured below.

CORE PROGRAM
Vertical Abs - Pike Lifts

Option #1 Pike Lifts - Passing Through a Tuck

1. Begin from hollow body hang.

2. Tuck your knees high into your chest.

3. Extend your legs into a pike. Keep your legs straight as you lower them to step 1.

Option #2 Full Pike Lifts

1. Begin from hollow body hang.

2. Keep your legs straight as you begin lifting them up into a pike.

3. Continue to lift as high as you can with straight legs. Lower with control.

CORE PROGRAM
Vertical Abs - Pike Lifts

WHY?
Pike Lifts work not only your core but your hip flexors and lats. They are a very powerful exercise that is a true testament to strength, control and flexibility.

TECHNIQUE TIPS & MODIFICATIONS
- Begin with option #1 and gradually work your way up to option #2, passing through a tuck is the less difficult option.
- Repeat 10x eventually working your way up to 2-3 sets of 10.
- Stretch your hamstrings well before doing this, flexibility in the back of the legs is an important component to the success of this exercise.
- Legs remain engaged and straight during the full pike lifts, no bent knees allowed!
- Keep your feet pointed throughout. Pointing your feet helps you to connect and engage the muscles in your legs, loose feet will actually make it harder to keep your legs straight.
- If you feel this in your lower back try tucking your pelvis under, you may be slightly arching and using your lower back instead of your core and hip flexors.
- The power of the leg lifts comes from not only your core but your lats (the muscles on the side of your back). Think of pressing down with your lats to lift your legs even higher.
- If you feel yourself swinging you are most likely using momentum. Try slowing down and avoid swinging your legs to lift them up, instead control each lift from your core (I know, it's so hard!).
- Once you can perform the exercise with excellent form and control, option to add ankle weights!

CORE PROGRAM
Vertical Abs - Straddle Scissors

1. Begin from hollow body hang.

2. Maintain straight legs as you lift them open into a straddle.

3. Close your legs crossing one ankle on top of the other.

4. Open your legs back to straddle.

5. Close your legs crossing your other ankle on top.

6. Open back to a straddle. Repeat 3-5x with each ankle on top.

CORE PROGRAM
Vertical Abs - Straddle Scissors

WHY?

Straddle Scissors strengthen your core, hip flexors and front of your thighs. Each time you open into the straddle you are stretching your inner thighs. In order to gain the benefits your legs must be turned out and straight.

TECHNIQUE TIPS & MODIFICATIONS

- Stretch your straddle on the floor prior to doing this.
- Do your best to keep your legs lifted to 90 degrees the entire time, especially when you cross your legs in front of you.
- Be sure to alternate the leg that is on top during your scissors.
- You may feel the tops of your thighs cramp up when attempting this exercise, which is normal. This will happen less and less as your strength increases.
- Quality over quantity, if you feel you are losing your form stop and rest and try again, this is a challenging exercise.
- Option to perform Straddle Scissors while doing a Chin-Up Hold.

CORE PROGRAM
Vertical Abs - Front Kicks

1. Begin from hollow body hang.

2. Lift one leg up to the front as high as you can keeping it straight and slightly turned out.

3. Scissor your legs past each other and lift your opposite leg up. Repeat 5-10x on each leg.

Warm up with the Single Straight Leg Stretch

CORE PROGRAM
Vertical Abs - Front Kicks

WHY?
Front kicks work your core and mobility in your legs. They resemble grand battements in ballet only you're hanging!

TECHNIQUE TIPS & MODIFICATIONS
- Warm up for this exercise with the Single Straight Leg Stretch (page 33).
- When lowering each leg down pay attention that it doesn't go behind you, the leg shouldn't pass your starting hollow body position.
- Maintain slight turn-out in the legs to avoid gripping in the quads to lift the leg up.
- If you feel your hips popping or clicking engage your glutes tighter to give your hip more support.
- Do your best to stay still in your upper body as your legs lift.
- Start with the legs low and gradually work your way up to lifting them higher as pictured below.

LOWER BODY PROGRAM

Dancers legs are beautiful. They are strong in look, functionality and performance. Getting there is not an overnight process. Most professional ballerinas began at an early age, often 3 to 4 years old. Those that stick with the mundane process of repetitively learning the basics will, over time, naturally develop strength and endurance in the lower body. However, determination to reach beyond the norm when it comes to training techniques have shown, you **can** acquire legs similar to those of a seasoned ballet dancer. While some studies indicate genetics is also part of the equation, practice, practice and more practice is key.

The following images are designed to introduce you to proper positions and movements associated with ballet. Though individual results can and will be unique to each person, the practice of these ballet methods are helpful in gaining strength, endurance and flexibility needed to assist in **performing beautifully** in the world of aerial.

LOWER BODY PROGRAM
Supine Leg Lifts

1. Begin on your back with your arms reaching by your sides. Bend one knee placing your foot flat on the mat, extend your opposite leg up. Slightly turn out your extended leg and point your foot.

2. Maintain still in your hips as you lower your extended leg forward. Elongate your entire leg as you lift it back to your starting position. Repeat 10x on each leg.

If you managed to stay still in your hips and torso move on to steps 3 & 4.

3. Begin laying on your back with your arms reaching by your sides. Elongate one leg on the mat and extend your other leg up. Both legs are slightly turned out from your hips.

4. Maintain slight turnout and stillness in your torso and hips as you lower your leg in front of you. Think of reaching your leg further away from you to lift it back to your starting position. Repeat 10x on each leg.

LOWER BODY PROGRAM
Supine Leg Lifts

WHY?

Supine Leg Lifts are beneficial for lengthening and strengthening the leg in the hip joint. They also help you to become aware of maintaining stillness in your hips and torso as your legs move, which is beneficial for the ballet exercises to come!

TECHNIQUE TIPS & MODIFICATIONS

- Hold your leg steady at the top of each repetition, feel your abs holding the weight of your extended leg.
- Don't forget about your support leg! Keep your foot firmly pressing into the mat during step 1 or center your leg and reach it long in front of you during step 3.
- Reach your fingertips forward and press your palms into the mat to help you stabilize.
- Maintain slight turn-out of the lifted leg to avoid your quadriceps taking over for your abs and inner thigh muscles. Think about lengthening out of the front of the hip and engage your lower glutes to help maintain your turn-out.
- Don't lower your leg so low in front of you that your back arches off the mat.
- Slightly drop your chin to your chest to maintain length in the back of your neck.
- Start with steps 1 & 2, as you gain more stability move onto steps 3 & 4, once you've mastered that, add ankle weights for more challenge.

LOWER BODY PROGRAM
Side Leg Kicks - Up/Down

1. Lie on one side with both legs together and slightly forward of your trunk. Legs are turned out and feet are pointed. Place one hand behind your head and the other on the mat in front of your waist.

2. Lift your top leg up as high as you can, maintaining a straight turned out leg while staying still in your torso. Resist and lengthen your leg as you lower. Repeat 10x on each leg.

"A year from now you may wish you had started today."
-Karen Lamb

LOWER BODY PROGRAM
Side Leg Series - Up/Down

WHY?

The Up/Down Side Leg Kicks target the hips, glutes and outer thighs. This exercise is also a dynamic stretching method and helps to improve flexibility and range of motion in your inner thighs and hips. The goal is to remain still in your torso as your leg moves up and down with control.

TECHNIQUE TIPS & MODIFICATIONS

- Maintain your turn-out as you lift the leg up and down to avoid overworking the quadriceps.
- Keep your waist long on each leg kick, do your best not to shorten or sink between your ribs and your hips.
- Look straight forward and lengthen the back of your neck.
- Elongate your leg from your hip, imagine your top leg is growing longer than your bottom leg on the way down.
- Don't forget about your abs! Even though the focus is on the legs, the abs must always stay pulled in and up to support you.
- For an added challenge place both hands behind your head with wide elbows.
- Once you've mastered steps 1 & 2 with complete control, try adding ankle weights for more challenge.

LOWER BODY PROGRAM
Side Leg Series - Front/Back

1. Lie on one side with both legs together and slightly forward of your trunk. Legs are turned out and feet are pointed. Place one hand behind your head and the other on the mat in front of your waist.

2. Lift your top leg up to hip height maintaining very slight turn-out. Keep your waist long and your torso still, as you swing your leg to the front with a flexed foot. Once you reach your maximum height do 2 small pulses.

3. Reach long out of your hip as you sweep your leg behind you with a pointed foot and again do 2 small pulses. Repeat 10x on each leg.

LOWER BODY PROGRAM
Side Leg Series - Front/Back

WHY?

The Front/Back Side Leg Kicks help to develop core stability and balance. In addition they work your glutes and hip abductors. This exercise is also considered a dynamic stretching method and helps to improve flexibility in your hamstrings and hip flexors.

TECHNIQUE TIPS & MODIFICATIONS

- Do not let your shoulders or hips rock forward and back as your leg moves.
- Think about maintaining the same distance between the top of your hip and your ribcage the entire time, no sinking in the waist allowed!
- The pulses add a dynamic hamstring stretch when the leg is forward.
- When the leg is to the back it serves as a hip flexor stretch for the top hip.
- Maintain slight turn-out the entire time to ensure your quadriceps don't do all of the work.
- Imagine you have a cup of tea balancing on your top shoulder, don't let it spill as you swing your leg front and back.
- The hip flexors (psoas) is stretched when the leg reaches to the back. Frequent sitting can cause tight hip flexors, hamstrings and lower back. This exercise serves as a dynamic stretch which can improve overall posture.
- For an added challenge place both hands behind your head with wide elbows.

LOWER BODY PROGRAM
Side Leg Series - Side Passé

1. Lie on one side with both legs together and slightly forward of your trunk. Legs are turned out and feet are pointed. Place one hand behind your head and the other on the mat in front of your waist.

2. Lift your top leg as high as you can maintaining your turn-out and length in your waistline.

3. Bend your knee to passé by placing your toes near the inside of your bottom knee. Slide your toes down the lower part of your leg until your leg is straight. Repeat 5-10x and reverse the direction. Bend the knee first followed by extending the leg.

LOWER BODY PROGRAM
Side Leg Series - Side Passé

WHY?

The Side Passé targets the inner and outer thighs as well as the hips. It's a great preparation exercise for the ballet barre passé exercise to come.

TECHNIQUE TIPS & MODIFICATIONS

- Maintain length in your waist as your top leg lifts and bends.
- Keep your hips stacked and level while drawing your leg into the passé position.
- Reach your top leg away from you as you lower it down.
- Keep your neck long and gaze straight forward throughout.
- Passé is pronounced (pah-say) meaning 'passed' in ballet terminology.

LOWER BODY PROGRAM
Prone Glute Lift

1. Lie down facing the mat. Place your hands one on top of the other and rest your forehead down. Bend your knees and bring your heels together with pointed feet. Knees are open hip distance apart.

2. Draw your abs in and away from the mat. Lift your thighs off the floor by squeezing the back of your legs and glutes. Hold your legs up for 3-6 seconds. Lower down with control and repeat 20x. Option to lift your legs to their highest point, lower slightly and press back up and pulse up and down for 20-30 pulses.

LOWER BODY PROGRAM
Prone Glute Lift

WHY?
Prone glute lifts strengthen and sculpt the glutes and backs of the upper legs.

TECHNIQUE TIPS & MODIFICATIONS
- Avoid arching your lower back, doing so will result in shortening your deep hip flexors and tighten your lower back. Instead, pull your abs in and up away from the floor during the entire exercise. Your pelvis should remain neutral and still throughout.
- Keep your knees open hip distance apart as you lift up and down.
- Relax your shoulders and neck throughout.
- Target the hamstrings by flexing the feet instead of pointing.
- For more of a challenge add ankle weights.

LOWER BODY PROGRAM
Arabesque Lifts

1. Kneel with your knees under your hips and extend one leg behind you slightly turned out. Hands under your shoulders with fingers facing forward. Scoop your abs in and up.

2. With a straight leg and pointed foot extend your outstretched leg up behind you without collapsing in your lower back.

3. Maintain still in your torso as you lower your leg about twelve inches.

4. Lift your leg back up as high as you can without collapsing in your lower back, repeat 20-30x.

LOWER BODY PROGRAM
Arabesque Lifts

WHY?
Arabesque lifts tone the glutes and strengthen your back. This exercise is a preparation for the arabesque at the barre.

TECHNIQUE TIPS & MODIFICATIONS
- Maintain a pulled in center to avoid arching your lower back.
- Keep your extended leg slightly turned out and straight the entire time.
- Keep your neck in alignment with the rest of your spine, do not allow your head to hang down.
- The foot remains pointed throughout.
- Your torso remains still the entire time, think of the upper body maintaining plank position as your leg extends behind you.
- Keep equal weight in your hands, it's common to shift your weight over to one side as your leg lifts.

LOWER BODY PROGRAM
Derrière Lifts

1. Begin kneeling on all fours. Hands underneath your shoulders and knees underneath your hips. Pull your abs in and up to lengthen your back.

2. Lift one leg up behind you to a 90 degree angle with a parallel leg and flexed foot.

3. Maintain still in your torso as you lower your leg about twelve inches.

4. Lift your leg up to your starting position targeting the muscles in the back of your upper leg.

Optional For an added glute challenge do the exercise with ankle weights.

LOWER BODY PROGRAM
Derrière Lifts

WHY?

Derrière Lifts work your glutes and hamstrings which result in a more lifted backside. Strong glutes help to support the lower back and posture.

TECHNIQUE TIPS & MODIFICATIONS

- Pull your abs in and up and front ribs together in step 1.
- Avoid sinking in your shoulders, instead press away from the floor.
- Keep your foot flexed to recruit the hamstrings.
- Begin with 10 lifts on each leg, work your way up to 30 lifts on each leg.
- Your torso remains still the entire time, think of the upper body maintaining plank position as your leg extends behind you.
- Keep equal weight in your hands, it's common to shift your weight over to one side as your leg lifts.
- Try lifting the leg to the side as pictured below.

LOWER BODY PROGRAM
Inner Thigh Lifts

1. Lie on your side with your top leg bent. Your knee and lower leg resting on the floor. Place your bottom hand behind your head and your opposite arm in front of your waist. Lengthen your bottom leg and bring it slightly forward of your torso.

2. Slightly turn out your leg and point your heel upwards. Lift your extended leg up, reaching long out of your hip. Lower the leg down without touching the mat and lift once again. Repeat 10x. Option to hold high at the top and do 10-20 small pulses. Switch legs.

"It is the mind itself which builds the body."
-Joseph Pilates

LOWER BODY PROGRAM
Inner Thigh Lifts

WHY?
Inner thigh lifts target your inner and outer thighs while giving the back of your hip a stretch.

TECHNIQUE TIPS & MODIFICATIONS

- Lift your leg up and down with control, imagine there is a book balancing on your heel, don't let it fall!
- Remain long and still in your torso as your leg lifts.
- Keep the back of your neck long, look straight forward and not down at your feet.
- Hips are stacked one on top of the other, do not allow your top hip to roll forward.
- Be sure not to bend your outstretched leg.
- Maintain a slight outward rotation of the leg to ensure the inner thigh does the lifting and not the quad.
- Once you achieve optimal form, add ankle weights for an added challenge.

LOWER BODY PROGRAM
Foot Positions in Ballet

Ballet Positions of the Feet

In the exercises to follow you will utilize some of the six foot positions pictured. Keep in mind the turn-out comes from the hips and not the feet themselves.

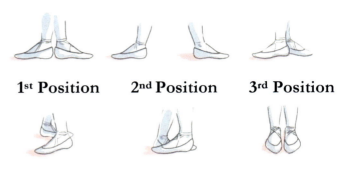

1st Position   2nd Position   3rd Position

4th Position   5th Position   6th Position

Directions & Proper Foot Placement

The positions below show the direction of the legs in ballet along with a proper pointed foot and an incorrect sickled foot. Sickling, as used in ballet and also aerial, refers to when the foot is misshaped in such a way that it is scooped down with the heel too far back. In a proper pointed foot the heel and ankle are slightly forward of the toes.

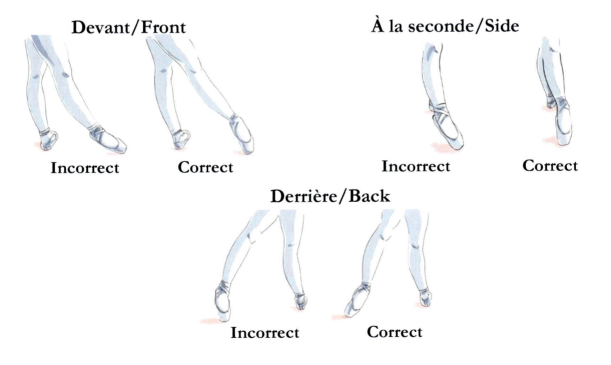

Devant/Front   À la seconde/Side

Incorrect   Correct   Incorrect   Correct

Derrière/Back

Incorrect   Correct

LOWER BODY PROGRAM
Proper Posture at the Barre

Anterior Pelvic Tilt
Lower Back Arching

Posterior Pelvic Tilt
Tucking Under
Shoulders Rounding
Forward

Neutral Alignment
Pelvis Level
Spine Lengthened
Shoulders Open

WHY?

Neutral alignment in our pelvis and spine is vital for the health and longevity of our bodies. When our body is aligned properly it functions better and we gain more benefits from exercise.

TECHNIQUE TIPS & MODIFICATIONS

- To attain neutral alignment draw your abs in and up while slightly drawing your tailbone down toward your heels (not so much that you are tucking under). Grow tall from the top of your head and widen your collar bones as you open the front of your chest.
- Neutral spine and neutral pelvis are different in every person, however they share the same elements. We want to preserve the natural and balanced curves of the spine when in neutral pelvis. When the pelvis is in its neutral position, it allows for the most amount of space between each vertebra. When there is space between each vertebrae the back is happy & healthy!
- Think of your pelvis as a bowl filled with soup, we don't want it to spill. Instead, it stays level so there is no spill at all!
- Keep your body well lifted or 'pulled up' you will find it easier to turn-out and lift your legs. It will also help you to appear lighter in your movements.

LOWER BODY PROGRAM
Foot Warm-Up

1. Begin facing the barre with feet parallel in 6th position. Lift the heel of your right foot pressing your arch forward.

2. Without lowering your right heel rise up onto the balls of your feet with straight and engaged legs. This is referred to as *demi-pointe* in ballet.

3. Lower your right heel down keeping your left heel lifted.

4. Lift both heels back up and repeat 20x.

LOWER BODY PROGRAM
Foot Warm-Up

WHY?
Your feet are your foundation. It's important that they are warmed up and stretched for the exercises to come.

TECHNIQUE TIPS & MODIFICATIONS
- Place your weight evenly on both feet when lifting your heels in step 2.
- Your weight should be evenly placed on your toes, do not lean more on your big or little toes.
- Maintain neutral alignment in your spine and pelvis.
- Lengthen your legs and grow tall in step 2 & 4, do not hyper-extend or push your knees back. Instead engage your low quadriceps (right above your knees) and think of pulling your muscles upwards.
- This exercise also serves as a stretch for your toes!
- Strong calf muscles help to extend the ankle joint, which occurs when you walk, run or jump.

"It is not the beauty of a building you should look at; it's the construction of the foundation that will stand the test of time."
-David Allen Coe

LOWER BODY PROGRAM
First & Second Position Demi-Pliés

1. Begin in neutral alignment with feet in first position. Place your inside hand on a chair or steady surface and your other hand on your hip.

2. Bend your knees while trying to increase the turn-out in your upper legs. Go as low as you can without lifting your heels. Squeeze your inner thighs together as you lengthen your legs. Repeat 10-20x.

Repeat the same exercise in 2nd position.

1. Begin in neutral alignment with feet in 2nd position.

2. Bend your knees as much as you can, maintaining your turnout and keeping your heels down.

LOWER BODY PROGRAM
First & Second Position Demi-Pliés

WHY?

Pliés (meaning *to bend*) are ideal for preparing and warming up your body for the more complex excises to come. They help to gain strength and elasticity in your legs and feet while giving you the opportunity to focus on your neutral alignment.

TECHNIQUE TIPS & MODIFICATIONS

- Feel a line through the length of your spine all the way up through the top of your head, this will help with stability and control. Imagine you are balancing a glass on your head, do not allow it to fall!
- Each time you bend your knees think about increasing your turn-out from the top of your thighs.
- Pay attention to not rolling inward or outward on your feet.
- Be sure to bend your knees as far as you can, keeping your heels down. Lifting the heels tightens your achilles tendon and doesn't allow for a stretch of your calves.
- When lengthening your legs feel your inner thighs and lower glutes draw together.
- Maintain neutral alignment in your pelvis and spine throughout.
- Keep your toes lengthened, do not allow them to grip the floor.
- For an added challenge and to work your glutes, thighs and calves remain in 2nd position, lift your heels up and down 10-20x.

LOWER BODY PROGRAM
Relevés & Leg Sculpting Exercises

1. Begin in neutral alignment with feet turned out from your hips in first position. Place your inside hand on a steady surface and your other hand on your hip.

2. Lift both heels off the floor at the same time arriving in relevé. Keep the muscles in your legs taut and pulled up while maintaining your turn-out. Lower your heels with control. Repeat 20-30x.

Plié Pulses

1. Rise up onto the balls of your feet and draw your heels together. Bend your knees into a demi-plié.

2. Maintain your turn-out from your upper thighs as you bend your knees deeper into your plié. Perform small pulses up and down. Repeat 20-30x.

LOWER BODY PROGRAM
Relevés & Leg Sculpting Exercises

2nd Position Heel Raises

1. Begin from a 2nd position plié.

2. Keep your knees bent as you lift your heels up. Lower with control. Repeat 20-30x.

WHY?

Relevés (meaning *to rise*) work your legs and feet. They add definition to your lower legs and improve your performance in many athletic pursuits. Plié pulses work to strengthen the ankles and inner and outer thighs.

TECHNIQUE TIPS & MODIFICATIONS

- Press away from the floor with the balls of your feet and grow tall from the top of your head on each lift.
- For optimal alignment and to improve support and ankle control avoid sickling your ankle. Instead focus on your relevé position being directly over the 2nd and 3rd toes.
- During the plie pulses watch that your knees don't roll in, instead keep your knees tracking over your 2nd and 3rd toes while maintaining your turn-out from your upper thighs.
- During the 2nd position heel raises think about your torso and head staying in the same place as your heels lift up and down.

LOWER BODY PROGRAM
Tendu & Dégagé

1. Begin from 1st position in neutral alignment with your legs pulled up and turned out from your hips.

2. Tendu Devant (Front)
Stretch your leg to the front leading with your heel and continuing with your toes. Close back to 1st, articulating through your foot.

3. Tendu à la seconde (Side)
Lengthen your leg to the side forming a straight line through your knee, instep & toes. Close back to 1st, articulating through your foot.

4. Tendu Derrière (Back)
Slide your leg behind you leading with your toes. Close back to 1st, articulating through your foot.

LOWER BODY PROGRAM
Tendu & Dégagé

Repeat the same front, side, back pattern lifting your foot a few inches from the floor performing dégagés. Articulate through your foot and squeeze your inner thighs together each time your legs join in 1st position.

WHY?

These two exercises help to improve your turn-out, warm-up your legs and build strength in your feet. Tendu means *stretched*. Dégagé means *disengage*, each time the foot lifts it *disengages* from the floor.

TECHNIQUE TIPS & MODIFICATIONS

- This exercise is not just about your working leg. Your supporting leg is just as important! Keep your supporting side lifted, leg turned out and muscles pulled up.
- Articulate through your foot on the way out and in.
- Be sure not to sickle your foot in any of the 3 positions (page 83).
- Keep your neck long and shoulders open.
- Turn-out from the top of your thigh as much as you can without shifting your pelvis.
- Lengthen the line of your leg by reaching out through your toes on each repetition.
- Repeat 2-3 sets of 4-8 in each direction, front/side/back/side - referred to as *en croix* in ballet.

LOWER BODY PROGRAM
Passé Développé Front & Side

1. Begin from 1st position in neutral alignment with your legs pulled up and turned out from your hips.

2. Draw a line up your leg with your toes while allowing your knee to bend to the side. Stop when your toes arrive to the outside of your knee forming a triangle shape known as *retire* in ballet.

3. Keep the top of your thigh lifted and turn-out out as you extend your leg to the front, hold for 3-5 seconds. Lower to 1st position with control.

4. Repeat steps 1-2 followed by extending your leg to the side. Hold for 3-5 seconds, lower to 1st position with control.

LOWER BODY PROGRAM
Passé Développé Front & Side

WHY?

Passé Développé is an unfolding movement of the leg. It helps to develop strength, balance, control and requires flexibility in the legs. Développé means *to develop* and passé means *to pass* in ballet terminology.

TECHNIQUE TIPS & MODIFICATIONS

- Stay lifted on your supporting side as you draw your leg up into passé, it's common to sink into the hip on the working leg.
- Keep your hips square and pelvis neutral the entire time.
- Stay long in your spine and firm in your abs throughout.
- Maintain the turn-out in your leg as you extend it to the front and side, if your leg turns in, the work happens from the quadriceps, which doesn't help create the *dancer lines* in your legs.
- Fully extend your legs and reach through your toes on each développé.
- Think of growing taller when you return to 1st position.
- Repeat 4-8x to the front and side.

INADEQUATE LEG EXTENSION

PROPER LEG EXENSION

LOWER BODY PROGRAM
Passé Développé Arabesque

1. Begin facing the barre. Draw a line up your leg with your toes while allowing your knee to bend to the side. Stop when your toes arrive to the inside of your knee forming a triangle shape known as *retire* in ballet terminology.

2. Stay lifted in your chest and maintain the turn-out from your hip as you unfold your leg behind you into an arabesque. Straighten your leg completely and fully point your foot. Hold for 3-5 seconds. Lower your leg down with control passing through tendu derrière and closing into 1st position. Repeat 4-8x on each leg.

LOWER BODY PROGRAM
Passé Développé Arabesque

WHY?

Arabesque works your hip extensors including your glutes, utilizes the muscles in your back and improves your balance. There are many different types of arabesques, some more difficult than others, facing into the barre is one of the more supportive options.

TECHNIQUE TIPS & MODIFICATIONS

- Keep your spine lengthened, your abs pulling in and up and your supporting leg turned out and straight.
- Allow your pelvis to tip forward slightly as your leg lifts behind you but not so far that your torso is no longer lifted.
- Place your hands lightly on the chair (or steady surface) in front of you. Feel equal weight in your hands as you lift your leg, this will help keep your shoulders square to the front.
- Be sure to fully extend your leg behind you and reach out long through your pointed foot, relaxed legs and feet are not allowed!
- As you build strength you will be able to lift your leg higher and higher, never comprise your form just to hike your leg up.
- If you feel the side of your lower back cramping as you lift your leg, don't worry, this is a normal sensation. Think of growing taller and rest if needed, the cramping will lessen as your strength improves.
- Once you feel confident with the exercise facing into the barre (or chair) try it sideways to the barre or without any support at all!

LOWER BODY PROGRAM
Attitude Lifts

1. Begin facing into the chair. Lift one foot off the floor with the knee out to the side. Place your pointed foot just below your calf muscle into *cou-de-pied* as pictured.

2. Keep your leg turned out from your hip as you lift your leg up behind you into an attitude.

3. Lower your leg about twelve inches.

4. Lift back up to your full attitude. Repeat 10-20 lifts on each leg.

LOWER BODY PROGRAM
Attitude Lifts

WHY?
Attitude Lifts are a great way to tone your back, glutes and legs. This exercise also works your balance and stability.

TECHNIQUE TIPS & MODIFICATIONS
- Keep your standing leg straight and pulled up the entire time.
- Think of your bent knee being higher than your toes, this prevents your knee from dropping and turning in.
- Allow your pelvis to tilt forward slightly as you lift your leg behind you.
- Stay engaged in your abdominals and relaxed in your shoulders and neck.
- Keep your gaze straight forward, not down.
- *Cou-de-pied* is a ballet term meaning on the *neck of the foot*.

> "The difference between ordinary and extraordinary is that little extra." *-Jimmy Johnson*

LOWER BODY PROGRAM
Grand Battements

1. Begin from 5th position with one hand on a chair. Pull up through your center and raise your outside arm as pictured or keep it on your hip.

2. Toss your leg to the front while maintaining your turn-out in both legs and a tall spine. Close your legs back to 5th position.

3. Open your arm to the side as you battement your leg to à la seconde. Close back to 5th position.

4. Reach your arm forward and lift your leg to the back keeping a straight leg and pointed foot. Return to 5th position.

LOWER BODY PROGRAM
Grand Battements

WHY?

Grand Battements tone the legs and increase dynamic movement and power. Battement means *to throw* in ballet terminology.

TECHNIQUE TIPS & MODIFICATIONS

- Be sure your legs are warmed up prior to doing this exercise.
- Keep your spine lengthened and abs drawing in and up.
- Pay attention to your supporting leg, be aware that it doesn't bend as your opposite leg lifts.
- Maintain your turn-out in both legs throughout, remember the turn-out happens from your hips, not your feet.
- Each time your leg leaves the floor allow it to draw back to 5th position while articulating through your foot.
- Watch that you don't stick out your tush, especially when lifting the leg to the side.
- If 5th position feels uncomfortable do 3rd position instead (see page 83 for foot positions).
- Option to keep your hand on your hip if the arm positions pictured are too much.
- When first starting you may not be able to lift your legs very high, that is ok! Form and posture is more important than how high your leg lifts.
- Repeat 3-6 grand battements in each direction, front/side/back/side- referred to as *en croix* in ballet.

UPPER BODY PROGRAM

Gaining upper body strength is vital in the aerial world. The muscles of the arms, chest, lats and back must be developed in order to climb and endure working aerial apparatuses such as silks, lyra, trapeze, straps and rope. Perhaps the number one exercise most associated with aerial is the chin-up and pull-up. These two systems work the entire upper body and will undoubtedly give you a sleek, yet strong torso and arms. To gain added strength and shapeliness, using free weights is helpful. The images and information in the following pages offer step-by-step instructions which will help you achieve the upper body you desire and the benefits of a strong, graceful body without the bulk.

UPPER BODY PROGRAM
Weight Work - Shoulders

1. Begin standing with feet hip distance apart and parallel. Draw your abs in and lengthen your spine. Hold one 2-5lb weight in each hand with your hands facing into your body.

2. Lift your arms to the front as high as you can without tensing in your neck.
Repeat 2-3 sets of 10.

3. Repeat the same steps above alternating arms.
Repeat 2-3 sets of 10 on each arm.

UPPER BODY PROGRAM
Weight Work - Shoulders

WHY?
This exercise targets and shapes the deltoid, which sits on top of the shoulder. Strong deltoids are important for skills such as hand-stands.

TECHNIQUE TIPS & MODIFICATIONS
- To work different parts of your deltoid - anterior (front), medial (middle) and posterior (rear) switch the direction of your hands so your thumbs point up instead of the palms facing you. Repeat the same patterns as pictured.
- Be aware that you are not tensing your neck or shrugging your shoulders to initiate the lift.
- The higher your arm lifts to the front the more tempting it is to arch the back, stay lifted in your center with your front ribs pulling together the entire time.
- Use 2-5lb weights, when the arms are fully extended it's best to use lighter weights to target the proper muscle group. If the weights are too heavy, the surrounding muscle groups may kick in to help out.
- Watch that you don't hyper extend your knees, keep your leg muscles pulling up and knees slightly soft (if you are a hyper-extender).

UPPER BODY PROGRAM
Weight Work - Triceps

Triceps Extension

1. Begin standing with feet hip distance apart, abs pulling in and up and spine long. Hold one weight overhead with your arms at a 90 degree angle.

2. Extend your forearms up keeping your elbows in the same place.

Triceps Lifts

1. Begin as pictured in a staggered lunge. Place a weight in your left hand and opposite hand on your hip.

2. Keep your arm straight and lift it high up behind you.

3. Lower your arm a few inches.

4. Lift back up. Repeat 20-30 lifts. Switch arms.

UPPER BODY PROGRAM
Weight Work - Triceps

Triceps Kickback

1. Begin as pictured in a staggered lunge. Place a weight in your left hand and place your opposite hand on your hip. Bend your left elbow to a 90 degree angle. Raise your upper arm until it is parallel to the floor.

2. Keep your abs tight as you extend your forearm behind you until your arm is straight. Hold and squeeze the back of your upper arm. Return to your starting position. Repeat 2-3 sets of 10 on each arm.

WHY?

Firmness of the upper arm is important to many. These exercises will tighten and tone the targeted area. If you are an aerialist your triceps are used all the time, it is crucial they are strong to support you!

TECHNIQUE TIPS & MODIFICATIONS

- In the staggered lunge position keep your spine long and bend forward from the hips. Bending forward at the hips allows you to get your arm up high behind you, making the exercise more effective.
- In all triceps exercises pay attention you are not tensing your neck to initiate the lift.
- In Triceps Lifts and Triceps Kickback your back foot is placed on an angle with the outside of your foot pressing firmly into the mat.
- Keep your neck in alignment with the rest of your spine throughout, make sure you are not allowing your head to drop forward.

UPPER BODY PROGRAM
Weight Work - Biceps

1. Stand with your feet hip distance apart, parallel with knees soft. Hold a weight in each hand. Bend your right elbow lifting the weight toward your shoulder. Squeeze your upper arm at the top.

2. Switch sides, bend your opposite arm and lengthen the other. Repeat 2-3 sets of 10.

WHY?

Biceps are a large muscle on the front of the upper arm. They work during day-to-day activities including lifting and carrying items. They are important for your pull-ups and chin-ups in the exercises to come.

TECHNIQUE TIPS & MODIFICATIONS

- This is a simple yet effective exercise, since your arms are not extended and straight you can use a heavier weight 5-10lbs.
- Maintain your posture and alignment throughout.
- Option to bend both arms at the same time instead of alternating.

UPPER BODY PROGRAM
Weight Work - Rotator Cuff

The Scarecrow

1. Begin standing with feet hip distance apart, parallel with knees soft. Place one weight in each hand. Lift your elbows open to the sides forming a 90 degree angle with each arm in external rotation.

2. Keep your elbows in the same place as you lower your forearms until you create a 90 degree angle the other direction in internal rotation.

3. Return to step 1 moving from internal to external rotation of the shoulders.

UPPER BODY PROGRAM
Weight Work - Rotator Cuff

External Rotation

1. Begin standing with feet hip distance apart, parallel with knees soft. Place one weight in each hand. Hug your elbows into your waist with your thumbs facing up.

2. Keep your elbows hugging into your waist as you open your forearms away from your body. Pause and feel the muscles around your shoulder blades squeeze together.

3. Return to your starting position.
Repeat 2-3 sets of 10.

UPPER BODY PROGRAM
Weight Work - Rotator Cuff

WHY?

The rotator cuff is made up of four muscles, the supraspinatus, infraspinatus, teres minor and subscapularis. These four form a 'cuff' of muscle and tissue around the shoulder joint, and are involved with the rotation of the arm in the shoulder. It is a commonly injured area due to the role it plays in arm movement. Perform these exercises regularly to keep your rotator cuffs healthy and injury free!

TECHNIQUE TIPS & MODIFICATIONS

- A common rotator cuff injury is shoulder impingement - the tissue of the shoulder joint can become inflamed and the rotator cuff can tear. Muscles or the tendon of the rotator cuff can also be injured. These injuries usually occur due to heavy lifting with improper form, misalignment and overuse.
- In both exercises maintain a lengthened spine and abs pulling in and up.
- In the Scarecrow exercise do not allow your elbows to drop as you externally and internally rotate your arms.
- In the External Rotation exercise keep your elbows glued to your waist the entire time.
- Both exercises can be a challenge even without weights. Choose an amount of weight that feels right for you.
- Do these exercises regularly to keep your shoulders healthy and strong!

UPPER BODY PROGRAM
Weight Work - Lats

Lat Rows

1. Begin standing with your feet parallel, hip distance apart, knees bent. Bend forward from your hips keeping your spine straight. Hold weights in your hands with palms facing in.

2. Draw your shoulders down and together as you bend your elbows until they are parallel to the floor forming a 90 degree angle by your waist. Hold for 2-3 seconds.

3. Lower your arms to your starting position. Repeat 2-3 sets of 10.

Lat Pull Over

1. Lie on your back with your knees bent. Weights in your hands, and palms facing up. Reach your arms back as far as you can without losing your abdominal connection.

UPPER BODY PROGRAM
Weight Work - Lats

2. Draw your shoulder blades down your back as you engage your lats to reach your arms up.

3. Extend your arms back overhead. Repeat 2-3 sets of 10.

WHY?
Your lats (latissimus dorsi) are a group of large muscle in your back that creates a V shape along the sides of your body. These exercises strengthen and tone giving you the look of a slimmer waistline.

TECHNIQUE TIPS & MODIFICATIONS
- Training the lats gives you more power in a lot of activities, if you are an aerialist they are your 'wings' that help to support you while in the air.
- Working the lats helps to improve your posture and prevent hunching the upper body forward.
- Keep your spine and the back of your neck long throughout each exercise.
- In the Lat Row position, initiate the movement by drawing your shoulder blades together while keeping your elbows close to your waist as you bend.
- In the Lat Pull Over keep your front ribs knitting together the entire time.
- Depending on the range of motion in your shoulders you may not be able to reach your arms as far as pictured in the Lat Pull Over, that is ok, proper form is more important than range of motion for this movement.
- For the Lat Rows you may be able to use a heavier weight than the Lat Pull Over due to the arms position, choose what suits you best!

UPPER BODY PROGRAM
Push-Ups

1. Begin in a plank position with your hands directly under your shoulders and finger tips facing forward. Press away from the floor, draw your abs in and up.

2. Keep your center engaged as you bend your elbows towards your waist forming a 90 degree angle.

3. Press away from the floor and arrive back in your plank position. Repeat 10x working up to 3 sets of 10.

UPPER BODY PROGRAM
Push-Ups

WHY?
Push-ups work the shoulders, chest, arms and upper back.

TECHNIQUE TIPS & MODIFICATIONS
- Keep your hips lifted in line with your shoulders, do not allow your hips to sink. Doing so will put a lot of pressure on your lower back. Instead, draw your abs in and up and slightly draw your tailbone down toward your heels.
- Bending the elbows in toward your waist puts less pressure on your shoulders than other push up options. It also targets your triceps.
- Don't allow your head to hang down as you push-up, keep your neck long and in alignment with the rest of your spine.
- If you have an injured shoulder, elbow or wrist, you may want to avoid this exercise as it may cause further injury.
- If it's too difficult to perform push-ups from a full plank position modify and lower to your knees as pictured below.

UPPER BODY PROGRAM
Grip Strengthener

1. Begin seated or standing in a comfortable position with your spine long. Reach your arms overhead and close your hands into tight fists.

2. Open your hands as wide as you can spreading your fingers apart (think *jazz hands*!).
Continue to open and close your hands tightly for 60-90 seconds.

WHY?
This exercise can be done anywhere and it's excellent for strengthening your grip and forearms. A MUST BE STRONG area for aerialists!

TECHNIQUE TIPS & MODIFICATIONS
- You should feel your forearms begin to burn after 20-30 seconds, try to push through the discomfort and work your way up to 60-90 seconds.
- Be sure you use the full range of motion, closing very tightly and opening as wide as you can to get the full benefits of the exercise.

UPPER BODY PROGRAM
Chin-Up & Pull-Up Grip

**Pull-Up Grip
Hands Face Out**

**Chin-Up Grip
Hands Face In**

WHY?

Both the pull-up grip and chin-up grip are necessary hand positions for the exercises to come. The pull-up grip works the triceps and lats when performing a pull-up. The chin-up grip focuses more on the biceps when performing a chin up. For most the pull-up grip will be more difficult than the chin-up grip due to the fact the lats and triceps do most of the work and not the biceps.

UPPER BODY PROGRAM
Shoulder Shrugs

1. Begin hanging in hollow body position with hands facing out with straight arms.

2. Maintain hollow body in your torso as you slowly relax your shoulders allowing them to shrug by your ears.

3. Keep your arms straight as you pull your shoulder blades down your back using your lats and surrounding muscles. Hold for 2-3 seconds before releasing. Repeat 1-2 sets of 10.

WHY?
Shoulder shrugs are a great warm-up and preventative exercise for shoulder injuries. They also work your grip and forearms which are vitally important in aerial!

TECHNIQUE TIPS & MODIFICATIONS
- Draw your abs in and knit your ribcage together in the front throughout.
- Keep your chin level and the back of your neck long.
- Arms must be straight throughout, it's tempting to bend the elbows in step 3, do your best to pull your shoulders down by using your back muscles.

UPPER BODY PROGRAM
Chin-Up Hold

1. Begin standing on a chair to make it easier to reach the bar. Place your hands on the bar slightly wider than shoulder distance with hands facing towards you.

2. Pull your chin above the bar, draw your elbows into your sides and maintain hollow body position. Hold for as long as you can with proper form eventually working up to 30-60 seconds. When you can no longer hold carefully step back onto the chair. Repeat 2-3 holds.

WHY?

The Chin-Up Hold is an excellent strength builder to work your way up to doing full pull-ups and chin-ups. When you're a beginner holding for five seconds may feel like an eternity! With regular practice your strength will increase and holding for longer will become easier.

TECHNIQUE TIPS & MODIFICATIONS

- If a chair doesn't suit your needs, find a steady object that will allow you to reach the bar and easily pull your chin above it.
- Keep your legs together, abs engaged and neck long throughout.
- Watch that you don't allow your body to sway, hold everything tight and together.

UPPER BODY PROGRAM
Negative Chin-Ups & Pull-Ups

1. Start in a chin-up hold position (as described on page 118). Hold at the top for a few seconds.

2. Begin to lower down slowly with control over the course of 10-15 seconds.

3. Continue to lower, take your time.

4. End with arms straight in a hollow body hang. Carefully release your grip and step back onto the chair. Repeat 5-10x. Switch to a chin-up grip.

UPPER BODY PROGRAM
Negative Chin-Ups & Pull-Ups

WHY?

Negative Chin-Ups and Pull-Ups increase your strength and power to eventually be able to do a full pull-up/chin-up. The key is to move very slowly as you lower down to gain the most benefits, eventually taking an entire 30 seconds to lower!

TECHNIQUE TIPS & MODIFICATIONS

- The main goal of this exercise is to move slowly, not just dropping down to straight arms, this is when the strength building really happens.
- Negative chin-ups mainly work your upper and mid back, biceps, forearms and core.
- To truly work your core efficiently in this exercise, think of pulling your abs in to stabilize your torso and spine. As you focus on lowering slowly, your abs kick in to minimize any swinging or arching in your lower back.
- Full range of motion is key here for developing long, lean, healthy muscles. Make sure you lower to fully straight arms, on each rep.
- Watch that you don't allow your shoulders to shrug by your ears on the descent (this will over-work and tighten your trapezius muscles around your neck) be very aware of pulling your shoulder blades down.
- Be sure to switch your grip and do the same exercise using a pull-up grip as pictured below.

UPPER BODY PROGRAM
Assisted Pull-Ups & Chin-Ups

1. Loop a large superband around a pull-up bar. Place one knee or foot at a time into the band and reach your hands up to the bar. Grab the bar with a pull-up grip.

2. Allow the band to assist you as you pull your chin above the bar. Be sure to keep your abs in and ribs together in the front.

3. Begin to lower down with control.

4. Continue to lower.

5. End with your arms lengthened. Repeat 5-10x. Switch to a chin-up grip.

UPPER BODY PROGRAM
Assisted Pull-Ups & Chin-Ups

WHY?
The superband around the bar helps to lift some of your weight, that way you can practice your pull-ups and chin-ups using your full range of motion but with assistance. Over time, you won't need the band!

TECHNIQUE TIPS & MODIFICATIONS
- Pulling up is just as important as lowering down, do your best to make the most of each movement.
- Do not use momentum to pull your body up, this only cheats you out of gaining strength in the long run.
- When you begin the pull-up watch that you don't arch your lower back, instead pull your front ribs together.
- Don't allow your shoulders to shrug when pulling up and lowering down, this will over-work your trapezius and lead to strengthening the wrong muscles.
- When you're new to doing these exercises try 2-3 sets of 3-5 reps and work your way up to doing more. Even if it's only one, it's a start!

UPPER BODY PROGRAM
Pull-Ups & Chin-Ups

1. Begin hanging in hollow body position in a chin-up or pull-up grip.

2. Initiate the pull by drawing your shoulders down your back to bend your elbows.

3. Continue to pull up until your chin is above the bar.

4. Lower down with control.

5. Finish with straight arms in hollow body hang. Begin with 1 rep working your way up to 10+.

UPPER BODY PROGRAM
Pull-Ups & Chin-Ups

WHY?

Pull-ups and chin-ups are the ultimate upper body strength building exercises. For some they seem impossible to achieve! With proper practice of the exercises in this book, you will be fully prepared to conquer them!

TECHNIQUE TIPS & MODIFICATIONS

- The chin-up is usually easier to achieve than a pull-up, the different grips activate different muscles in your upper body. Chin-ups activate more of the biceps while pull-ups work more of the muscles in your back and triceps.
- Pulling up is just as important as lowering down, do your best to make the most of each movement.
- Do not kick your legs to help you lift your body. Maintain hollow body and pull yourself up using control.
- Keep your legs firm and pressing together to help stabilize.
- If your pull-up bar is at a height that you cannot fully straighten your legs then bend your knees, just be sure you don't lose your abdominal connection and lengthened spine.
- When you begin the pull-up make sure that you don't arch your lower back. Instead, pull your front ribs together.
- Don't allow your shoulders to shrug when pulling up and lowering down, this will over-work your trapezius and lead to ineffective movements.
- Do the same exercise with your hands in a pull-up grip.
- Start with the goal of doing one pull-up, one is a huge achievement!

STRETCHING PROGRAM

Stretching improves flexibility, helps proper muscle function and is vitally important for posture. If we neglect to stretch on a regular basis it can lead to discomfort, injury and poor posture. It also helps to create space in our bodies for our organs to function properly and can relieve stress. Regular stretching can help balance muscle lengths, which aligns the body leading to beautiful posture and a healthy pain-free physique. Visit page 8 to learn about the 4 key methods of stretching, Static, Dynamic, Passive and Active.

STRETCHING PROGRAM
Supine Leg Stretches

1. Begin lying on your back. Extend one leg up and reach your other leg long on the floor. Loop a strap over the arch of you extended leg. Keep your leg straight and hips square as you pull your leg towards you stretching your hamstring.

2. Hold the strap in one hand as you open the leg to stretch your inner thigh. Keep your leg turned out from your hip and your opposite side pressing into the mat.

3. Switch hands, cross your leg over your body stretching the outside of your leg and glutes. Flex your foot for a deeper stretch.

4. Continue to allow your leg to cross over for an added lower back and glute stretch. Look to the opposite side of the leg that is stretching.

STRETCHING PROGRAM
Supine Leg Stretches

WHY?

Supine Leg Stretches improve flexibility in the legs and can relieve a tight lower back. Each position pictured stretches a different muscle group, all of which are vital to mobility, balance and health of your leg muscles. Flexibility in the legs helps improve your performance in a variety of activities, it is very important for aerial arts.

TECHNIQUE TIPS & MODIFICATIONS

- Make sure you have warmed-up prior to doing these stretches.
- Hold each stretch for 30-60 seconds.
- If you find it too difficult to keep your supporting leg straight on the mat bend your knee and place your foot down instead. This will allow you to keep length in your spine and proper placement of your pelvis, you never want to feel like you are straining to achieve a stretch.
- Engage the muscles on the front of your legs to stretch deeper through the back of the leg, this is referred to as active stretching.
- In step #2 it's not about how close to the floor you can get your leg. Instead, think about turning your leg out from your hip and aiming it towards your shoulder.
- Take deep breaths while stretching.
- Keep your shoulders and neck relaxed throughout.
- For an increased stretch flex your foot.
- If you don't have a yoga strap or resistance band use a towel or even a scarf to loop over your foot.

STRETCHING PROGRAM
Hip Flexor Stretch

1. Lie on your back. Hug one knee tightly in towards your chest while you reach the opposite leg away lengthening through the front of your hip. Hold for 30-60 seconds. Switch legs.

2. Option to add a yoga block
For an added stretch place a yoga block under the back of your hips. As you pull your knee into your chest reach your opposite heel away.

WHY?
The hip flexors are made up of five different muscles that connect the knee, the lower back and the hip to the pelvis. These muscles work frequently and are used in movements as simple as walking. In aerial, they work anytime we lift our legs while in the air. When they become weak or short (usually due to excessive sitting) they can compromise your body by pulling the front of your pelvis down causing an anterior pelvic tilt (lower back arch) which commonly leads to lower back pain. Moral of the story, if you have a tight lower back, stretch your hips!

TECHNIQUE TIPS & MODIFICATIONS
- Begin hugging your right knee in followed by your left, this helps to aid in digestion by pressing on your ascending colon followed by descending colon.
- Only add the block if you're not feeling an adequate stretch in step 1.
- Keep your hips square throughout.

STRETCHING PROGRAM
Seated Pike

1. Begin seated with your legs out in front of you. Spine long and arms reaching up.

2. Stretch forward over your legs keeping your spine long. Hold for 30-60 seconds.

3. Option to add a yoga block
For an added stretch place a yoga block in front of your feet, reach forward and grab on either side of the block.

STRETCHING PROGRAM
Seated Pike

WHY?

The Seated Pike stretches the muscles in the back of the legs. This area is a tight spot for the majority of the adult population due to frequent sitting. For aerialists the more open your hamstrings are, the better your pike, the easier many tricks and movements are.

TECHNIQUE TIPS & MODIFICATIONS

- This stretch is not about just trying to touch your toes. It's about maintaining the length in your spine to stretch your hamstrings.
- Avoid hunching in your shoulders.
- Stay lifted in your center and maintain length in your torso.
- Feet can be pointed or flexed, flexed feet increases the stretch down the back of your legs and calves.
- If you have very tight hamstrings try sitting on a yoga block followed by stretching forward. This allows you to keep more length in your spine.
- Another option if you cannot keep your spine long as you stretch forward, bend your knees as pictured below. This way you are actually stretching your hamstrings instead of straining and rounding your lower back to achieve the 'look' of the stretch. As your flexibility improves gradually work on straightening your legs.

STRETCHING PROGRAM
Straddle Stretch

1. To prepare begin seated tall in a 'butterfly' position with the soles of the feet together and knees open wide. Hold and breathe.

2. Open your legs wide into a V with your spine long, leg straight and toes pointing up.

3. Turn your torso to the side, place one hand on either side of your leg. Hold and breathe, switch sides.

4. Place your forearm down in front of you, extend your opposite arm up overhead and stretch to the side. Hold and breathe, switch sides.

STRETCHING PROGRAM
Straddle Stretch

5. Stretch forward hinging from the hips. Keep your legs turned out from your hips and your spine long during the stretch.

WHY?

The Straddle targets your inner thighs along with a slight stretch in your back, calves and hamstrings. As you stretch to either side, you'll feel it in your obliques and quadratus lumborum (back muscle). The straddle is a vitally important position for aerial, it is the base of many movements and tricks.

TECHNIQUE TIPS & MODIFICATIONS

- If you cannot sit up tall in a wide V, bring your legs closer together.
- Hold each stretch for 30-60 seconds.
- Keep your spine long in each position, excessive rounding is not healthy for your back, nor will it be a productive stretch.
- When you stretch to the side in steps 3 and 4 keep your opposite side down (the tush likes to lift off the floor).
- Keep your feet either pointed or flexed, flexing adds a calf stretch while pointing works the muscles in your legs and feet.
- For an active stretch tighten the muscles in the front of your thighs (your quads) and hold for 20-30 seconds, release and notice you'll be able to relax deeper into your stretch.
- When stretching to the side in step 4 reach long out of your top arm all the way through your fingers to get the most of out the stretch.
- When stretching forward in step 5 do not allow your legs to turn in.

STRETCHING PROGRAM
Middle Splits

1. Prep for the middle split by stretching in a 'frog' position. To get in position kneel with your forearms on the mat. Gradually walk your knees open as wide as you can until your hips are in line with your knees. Widen your feet so your ankles are in line with your knees with your feet flexed to protect your ankles. Hold for 60 seconds and carefully ease out of the stretch.

2. Begin in a squat with your hands in front of you. Begin to press into your hands and walk your feet outwards.

3. Widen your legs as much as you can allowing your arms to support you. Your legs must remain straight, spine is long and hips are in line with your heels. Hold for 60 seconds.

STRETCHING PROGRAM
Middle Splits

WHY?

Middle splits is one of the most difficult yet impressive stretches. This stretch is intense on the inner thighs and hips. It involves the legs extending in opposite directions until they form a 180 degree angle. For some achieving a flat middle split is anatomically not in the cards, depending on the structure of the hips. Regardless, it still serves as an excellent stretch.

TECHNIQUE TIPS & MODIFICATIONS

- Be sure your legs are warmed up prior to attempting this stretch.
- If the frog stretch is painful on your knees place a blanket or towel underneath them. If you have a knee injury you may want to avoid the frog stretch all-together.
- Keep your legs completely straight and feet parallel as you lower yourself down into your middle split.
- In the middle splits you want your hips in line with your legs. If your hips are too far back or forward you will not be in the proper position.
- Remember to move slowly and breathe. Do not push yourself to the point of strain. You should feel stretch in your inner thigh and groin muscles, but it should not feel painful. If you feel any serious discomfort or tearing sensations, come out of the stretch immediately.
- Hold for 60-90 max. In some cases holding a stretch for too long can cause more harm than good. Due to the intensity of the stretch a 60-90 second hold is plenty.

STRETCHING PROGRAM
Split Preparation

1. HIP FLEXOR STRETCH Begin in a lunge position with your front leg at a right angle and your back knee and foot on the mat. Place your hands on your front thigh. Draw your abs in, elongate your spine and slightly drop your tailbone down. Squeeze your tush and you'll feel an added stretch in your front hip flexor.

2. QUAD STRETCH Keep your front leg at a right angle. Carefully bend your back knee as you reach to grab the front of the foot or shin. Gently pull your heel towards your tush.

3. HAMSTRING STRETCH Lengthen your front leg, place your hands down on either side. Sit your hips back towards your heel. Keep your spine long and chest open. Option to place yoga blocks to either side of your front leg, if you have a difficult time reaching the floor.

STRETCHING PROGRAM
Split Preparation

WHY?

To achieve full splits it requires flexibility of the hip flexor and quad of the back leg and hamstring flexibility of the front leg. The three stretches pictured will help open up all the areas of the lower body necessary to achieve a full split.

TECHNIQUE TIPS & MODIFICATIONS

- In the hip flexor stretch the more you can keep your spine upright, your tailbone dropping down and the engagement of your glutes, the more effective stretch you will get.
- During the quad stretch make sure your knee cap isn't directly on the mat, think of your weight resting right above your knee on your lower quad. If it is painful place a towel underneath your back knee.
- In the hamstring stretch keep your front leg straight and flex your foot for a deeper sensation down the back of your leg.
- Do not allow your spine to round and shoulders to hunch.
- The blocks are used to raise the floor up to make it easier to lengthen your spine, when your spine is long the more anatomically correct the stretch is, therefore leading to better results.
- Hold each stretch for 30-60 seconds on both sides.

"Change happens through movement and movement heals."
-Joseph Pilates

STRETCHING PROGRAM
Front Splits

1. MODIFIED SPLIT Begin from the hamstring stretch pictured on page 136. Slide your legs apart into a split keeping your hips square to the front. Option to keep the blocks under your hands for a more upright and anatomically correct position if you are not fully down into your split.

2. FULL SPLIT With square hips extend your legs in opposite directions while maintaining an upright torso. For an added challenge reach your arms up.

3. OVER SPLIT If you can achieve a full split comfortably then you may want to begin working on over-splits. Place a yoga block underneath your front heel for an additional stretch.

STRETCHING PROGRAM
Front Splits

WHY?

Front splits are an impressive measure of flexibility. It is often a popular goal to be able to do the splits. Doing a successful front split requires a high amount of flexibility in the legs and hips. With a regular stretching routine of the proper muscles in their ideal alignment, a full split can be achieved. For aerialists a split is a must for achieving the beautiful desired lines while in the air.

TECHNIQUE TIPS & MODIFICATIONS

- Be sure you are warmed-up and have completed the split prep stretches on page 136.
- It is common to practice the splits with-out squaring the hips (especially for dancers). The benefits of stretching with square hips is you're actually stretching muscles, when the hips are not square you are stretching ligaments which won't help you gain more flexibility. When practicing with square hips you most likely won't be able to get as close to the ground (which feels frustrating!) but the stretch will be more effective in the long run in an effort to improve your flexibility.
- Keep your legs straight and feet pointed throughout.
- Feel all 5 of your back toes on the floor and avoid sickling your back foot.
- To increase your flexibility don't just 'hang-out' in your splits. Instead, actively engage your legs for 20-30 seconds, relax and allow yourself to ease deeper into your split, this is referred to as active stretching.
- The over-split is only for those who are comfortable in their full split, be very careful getting into and out of this stretch. Eventually add a block under the back foot also!
- For aerialists, in order to achieve an inverted full split in the air, you must have an over-split on the floor.

STRETCHING PROGRAM
Glute Stretches

1. Begin lying on your back. Bend your right knee and place your foot on the mat. Lift your left leg up, and cross your ankle above the knee forming a number 4 shape.

2. FIGURE 4 Reach your left hand through the open space created by your left leg and grab your right hand that is reaching around the outside of your right thigh. Pull your right knee into your chest. Feel the stretch on the outside of your left hip.

3. SUPINE COW STRETCH
Beginning from the Figure 4 stretch, cross your legs over one another until there is no gap between them, bring your knees into your chest. Flex your feet and grab your ankles, gently pull outwards.

STRETCHING PROGRAM
Glute Stretches

WHY?

Tight glutes are a result of not just a great booty workout but quite the opposite! Glutes become tight due to excessive sitting and in-activity. Tightness in this area often causes pain in the hips, knees or lower back. The glutes consist of 3 muscles: gluteus maximus, gluteus medius and gluteus minimus.

TECHNIQUE TIPS & MODIFICATIONS

- When pulling your knee toward your chest in step 2 & 3 don't allow your tailbone to curl off the mat or your head to lift. Instead, release your tailbone down to keep your spine long and in proper alignment.
- Flex your feet, this helps to protect your knees and deepens the stretch.
- In step 2 you can place your foot on a wall instead of holding it in mid-air, this allows for a more supportive and restorative stretch.
- The stretches pictured also target a muscle called the piriformis, it is a small muscle that runs from your sacrum (back of your pelvis) to the outside of your upper thigh bone. If you have experienced sciatica (a tingling/nagging nerve sensation that runs down the back of the leg) do these stretches 3-4 times per day to help relieve it.
- Neglecting to stretch your glutes can lead to IT (Iliotibial) band issues, over time that can cause knee injuries and lower back pain.

STRETCHING PROGRAM
Cobra & Bow Pose - Shoulder Openers

Cobra

1. Lie face down on the mat with your hands directly underneath your shoulders. Legs are open hip distance apart with the tops of your feet pressing down.

2. Pull your abs in and up as you begin to lengthen your arms. Keep your chest open and shoulders drawing down your back. Reach the crown of your head forward. Lower with control. Repeat 4-8x.

Bow Pose

1. Lie face down on the mat. Bend your knees and bring your heels as close as you can towards your tush keeping your knees hip-distance apart. Reach back to the outside of your feet and hold onto your outer ankles.

2. Lift your feet upwards drawing your thighs off the mat. Your head, chest, and upper torso will also lift off the mat. Press your feet into your hands as you open the front of your chest. Hold for 20-30 seconds. To come out, gently lower your thighs to the mat and release your grip.

STRETCHING PROGRAM
Cobra & Up Dog - Shoulder Openers

WHY?

Both of these stretches open the chest and the front of the body. Opening up this area will prevent slouching and is a great way to regain balance after a lifestyle of rounding forward at desks, on the couch and in our cars. For aerialists, strong yet open shoulders are important!

TECHNIQUE TIPS & MODIFICATIONS

- The Cobra & Bow Pose are excellent for alleviating lower back pain. They open up the vertebrae allowing for more space and length in the spine.
- As difficult and odd as it may feel while lying face down, keep your abs drawing in and away from the mat to support your lower back.
- Do not allow your head to drop back, instead keep the back of your neck long and the crown of your head reaching forward in opposition.
- During the Bow Pose continually press your feet into your hands to stretch the shoulders, back and quads.
- Keep your legs open hip distance apart during Bow Pose to avoid compressing the lower back.

**Additional Shoulder Opener -
Wide Leg Forward Fold with Shoulder Stretch**

STRETCHING PROGRAM
Prone Shoulder Stretch

1. Lie face down with your arms extended to the sides at 90 degree angle from your trunk. Lift your right leg up and place your foot on the floor behind you. Keep the left side of your chest pressed to the floor and allow your right hand to support you. Hold for 30 seconds, switch sides.

2. For a deeper shoulder stretch bend your arms at a 90 degree angle with the elbow in line with the shoulder and palm flat. Hold for 30 seconds, switch sides.

WHY?
The prone shoulder stretch is a deep and effective shoulder and chest opener. You control how much stretch you gain by how much pressure you place onto the arm that is being stretched.

TECHNIQUE TIPS & MODIFICATIONS
- If you have a shoulder injury be cautious with this stretch.
- This stretch can be intense for some. Sticking with step 1 only will be plenty!
- If you are an aerialist this is a great pre and post practice stretch.

STRETCHING PROGRAM
Bridge

1. Begin lying on your back. Bend your knees, keeping your feet parallel and aligned with your hips. Draw your heels close to your tush. Reach your arms overhead and bend your elbows until you can place your palms flat on the floor on either side of your head. Be sure your elbows are pointing up and your fingertips are pointing toward your shoulders.

2. Press your feet into the floor and lift your hips up. Keep your feet and legs parallel. Press into your hands and lift your shoulders off the mat. Continue to press into your hands as you lift your head and gently place the crown of your head on the mat.

3. Straighten your arms and lift your head off the floor. Press down equally into your hands. Draw your chest forward and drop your tailbone down toward the back of your knees to lengthen rather than compress your lower back.
Hold at the top for 20-60 seconds.

STRETCHING PROGRAM
Bridge

4. Gently come out of the stretch by retracing your path. Bend your elbows, carefully place the crown of your head on the mat followed by your whole body. Rest on your back with your knees bent and dropped together. Repeat 2-3x.

WHY?

The Bridge (aka wheel, upward bow pose or urdhva dhanurasana) is a challenging move to execute properly. It opens and stretches the front of your body and strengthens your shoulders, back and arms. It's important to get in and out of it with control and correct alignment; otherwise, it's very easy to injure yourself!

TECHNIQUE TIPS & MODIFICATIONS

- If you've never done a bridge, please do not attempt it alone.
- Keep your elbows hugging toward the center line of your body.
- Keep your feet parallel. Turning your feet out may allow you to go into a deeper back bend but in return can compress your lower back and may cause injury over time.
- In all backbends, it's important to create space between your vertebrae. Imagine your spine lengthening with each breath instead of trying to fold in half backwards as much as you can.
- Option to deepen the backbend, walk your feet closer to your hands.

STRETCHING PROGRAM
Neck Stretch

1. Begin seated or standing in a comfortable position. Clasp your hands on the outside of your waist. Relax your shoulders and tilt your head to the side of your clasped hands. Breathe into the stretch. Hold for 30-60 seconds on each side.

WHY?
The neck is a tension spot for many. This stretch lengthens the muscles along the side of your neck while reliving stress with each breath.

TECHNIQUE TIPS & MODIFICATIONS
- For some, dropping the chin towards the shoulder while in this stretch is a nice relief for the outside of the neck.
- Make sure your shoulders are relaxing down equally.
- If you are an aerialist the neck muscles are involved more than we think, add this stretch into your warm-up and cool down routine.
- This stretch can be done virtually anywhere!

STRETCHING PROGRAM
Forearm Stretch

1. Begin kneeling with your toes tucked under. Place your hands on the mat with your fingers facing towards you. Press into your hands and begin to lean back until you feel a stretch in your forearms, wrists and fingers. Hold for 30-60 seconds.

WHY?

The forearms and wrists get tight from tasks such as typing, texting and planks, push-ups and pull ups. For aerialists this is your go-to stretch due to the amount you use your grip and forearms while in the air!

TECHNIQUE TIPS & MODIFICATIONS

- This stretch is great for carpal tunnel or other wrist mobility injuries.
- Keep your arms straight throughout.
- For aerialists you may need to do this stretch several times during your aerial practice to prevent 'Popeye' forearms!

ACKNOWLEDGEMENTS

The author, Jill Franklin, would like to thank the following people for their assistance with the production of this book:

Jasmin Yang - Model
Gabe Hilden-Reid - Model
Greta Kirber Beck - Model
Maddy Palafox - Makeup Artist
&
A Very Special Thank You To:
TC Franklin Photography
www.tcfranklinphotography.com

Aerial Physique offers teacher training programs and workshops worldwide as well as private and group classes at the Aerial Physique studio in Los Angeles, CA.

www.aerialphysique.com
www.shopaerialphysique.com
www.aerialphysique.tv

Contact Aerial Physique:
info@aerialphysique.com
1-800-208-2246